NATURAL EYE CARE

AN ENCYCLOPEDIA

NATURAL EYE CARE

AN ENCYCLOPEDIA

O

COMPLEMENTARY TREATMENTS FOR IMPROVING AND SAVING YOUR EYES

MARC GROSSMAN, O.D., L.AC.
GLEN SWARTWOUT, O.D.

KEATS PUBLISHING

LOS ANGELES

NTC/Contemporary Publishing Group

Natural Eye Care is not intended as medical advice. Its intent is solely informational and educational. Please consult a health professional should the need for one be indicated.

NATURAL EYE CARE
Copyright © 1999 by Marc Grossman and Glen Swartwout
All Rights Reserved

Library of Congress Cataloging-in-Publication Data

Grossman, Marc.
    Natural eye care, an encyclopdia : complementary treatments for improving and saving your eyes / Marc Grossman, Glen Swartwout.
        p.   cm.
    Includes bibliographical references and index.
    ISBN 0-87983-704-7
    1. Eye — Diseases — Alternative treatment — Encyclopedias.   2. Eye — Care and hygiene — Encyclopedias.   I. Swartwout, Glen.   II. Title.
III. Title : Natural eye care.
RE21.G76   1999
617.7—dc21   98-55416
                                                                              CIP

Printed in the United States of America

Keats Publishing

Contents

Foreword

The world is changing. Our concepts of Western medicine have shifted over the past several years, and we are demanding much more of our health care providers. The reductionist mentality of referring each symptom to the domain of a particular specialist, isolated from the whole person, is being replaced slowly with more complementary forms of health care. We are beginning to look at the whole person, his or her dietary preferences, exercise regimens, the types of relationships they are engaged in, as well as the particular symptoms that brought them in for treatment in the first place.

It has been my privilege and pleasure to have worked with Dr. Grossman for the past several years, and (pardon the pun), he has opened my eyes to seeing vision problems in an entirely new light. He believes that our eyesight doesn't happen in a vacuum, but rather has its roots in our total being, our genetic makeup, the food we eat, our work environment and exposure to airborne toxins, as well as our general belief systems about ourselves and the world we live in. Each of us is unique and literally takes the world in through our senses, primarily vision; moreover, the way we take in our world is, to some degree, a reflection of who we are and which symptoms we might manifest.

Using their broad background in optometry, nutrition, traditional Chinese and herbal medicine, Drs. Grossman and Swartwout give readers specific strategies for regaining control of their vision and their health in general. They address all manner of eye diseases, from dry eyes through glaucoma and macular degeneration and give specific easy-to-follow protocols with which readers can begin their own process of healing.

This exceptional book will open your eyes to the power that lies within you.

It will reconnect you to the basic truth that the body's own natural wisdom, given the right nourishment (beliefs, foods, herbs, supplements) will heal itself. *Natural Eye Care* offers a bridge where Western medicine and Eastern healing wisdom can come together to help the whole person heal, and more importantly, stay well.

— JASON ELIAS, M.A., L.AC., co-author of
The Five Elements of Self-Healing, Feminine Healing and
The A–Z Guide to Healing Herbal Remedies

Preface

Natural Eye Care offers a unique approach to improving vision from birth to old age, as well as a method for not only preventing vision problems but for understanding vision in its totality. Filled with the wisdom and insight of both ancient and modern-day healers, *Natural Eye Care* integrates the full range of alternative therapies as they apply to vision and vision disorders.

As a practical manual, this book will help you make safe, sensible choices in your vision care. Chapters devoted to major eye disorders, such as glaucoma, macular degeneration, cataracts and dry eyes, describe both the standard Western medical approach to treatment and the alternative methods, such as specific herbal remedies, acupressure points, nutritional advice (vitamin and mineral supplements), vision therapy and homeopathy.

You will learn about the underlying causes of common visual problems and be given tools and techniques to write your own prescription for healing. If a particular problem or cluster of symptoms indicates a need for more conventional treatment, you are given explicit, individualized guidance to help choose a doctor who will best meet your needs.

Vision problems are multiplying at epidemic proportions in our society. *Natural Eye Care* will show people how to become active participants in their own vision care, giving back the power and responsibility they have so trustingly handed over to their eye doctors. Our primary goal is to offer a practical approach to vision care based on an underlying philosophy that emphasizes prevention rather than cure. In doing so, we celebrate the healing power within all of us and the mind/body's inherent potential for self-healing.

The eye care industry is a multibillion dollar business. Glasses, contact lenses, eye surgery—the major tools of that industry—enter the lives of virtually all the citizens of the Western world. Aldous Huxley wrote in *The Art of Seeing* that "if everyone who had deficient vision had broken legs, the streets would be full of cripples."

Patients come in year after year, their eyesight getting worse. Conventional eye care professionals just give them stronger and stronger glasses. Something is wrong with this picture. Cataracts are present to some degree in nearly all adults over the age of 60. These patients are usually told, "Let's wait until the cataract 'ripens' (gets worse), and then we'll remove it surgically." Something is wrong with this picture. Patients with macular degeneration and glaucoma are told, "We'll watch it and try to keep it under control." Where is the much-needed prevention, education and rehabilitation? Something is wrong with this picture as well.

Natural Eye Care will educate readers about their vision difficulties, explain how to prevent vision disorders, and explore how they heal those that do occur. It will enable the individual to be a more informed consumer when it comes to vision care.

Medication and surgery may sometimes be necessary or even the appropriate way to maintain the precious gift of sight. This book and the approach it presents are intended to be used as an adjunct to these traditional treatments of vision problems.

Doctors in China have reached out to the West to borrow the best modern medicine can offer; we in the West can, in turn, take from the ancient wisdom of the East. By combining the medical approaches of East and West, we may be able to achieve better health with less cost.

Natural Eye Care will provide both the lay person and the eye care professional with a complementary, balanced approach. In the past, people's choices have been limited to either/or: either traditional medicine with its emphasis on health as a static state of well-being and disease as a breakdown or malfunction of the body machine, or alternative methods placing total emphasis on emotional, psychological or spiritual healing.

Natural Eye Care is dedicated to the belief that a common ground can be created in which the strengths of modern-day Western medicine can be united with the preventive approach of other healing modalities.

Acknowledgments

I would like to thank my teachers, colleagues, patients, friends and family for their love and support. Special thanks to:

- My optometric family Drs. Sam Berne, Ray Gottlieb, Robert Michael Kaplan, Jacob Liberman, my co-author Glen Swartwout and others too numerous to mention with special indebtedness to my two primary mentors, Drs. Albert Shankman and Elliot Forrest.
- My office colleagues who make working with patients such an enjoyable experience: Dr. Bob Lesnow, Katy Bray, Vinton McCabe, Denise Catuguno, Annette Nacinovich, Kim Pitcher, Dr. Mark Fillipi, Dr. Ron Wish and Dr. Catherine Sweet. Special thanks to my friend, mentor and partner at Integral Health Associates, Jason Elias, for his inspiration and help.
- My community of friends whose nourishment I feel everyday: Michael Edson, Ellen Marshall, Amy Fradon, Loren Quimby, Bea Ehrsam, Pasquale Strocchia, Paul Barone, Hindy Preskin and David Lester.
- Carol Lorente for her wonderful gift for turning our ideas into the written word.
- Ramona Fradon for illustrations, Katy Taylor for endless patience as copywriter and Phyllis Herman, our editor, for her belief in the concept of natural eye care.
- My wonderful parents, sisters and their families, Dorothy and Irwin Grossman; Karen, Ronald, Cory and Jenna Speicher; Lisa, Scott, Steven and Jessica Ente.
- Finally, my departed grandmother, Esther Teichman, whose failing eyesight inspired me to help others with their vision.

—MARC GROSSMAN

Introduction

To See

When he broke that commitment to art, to making beauty, to recording, to bearing witness, to saying yessiree to the life spirit, whose only request sometimes is just that you acknowledge you truly see it, he broke something in Hal. Hal could not defend himself, for instance; he didn't consider himself worthy of defense. He never learned to fight. And listen, the most amazing thing, his eyes became weak! But I always took up for him, I knew he had to be reminded that it was all right to see.

—ALICE WALKER, *THE TEMPLE OF MY FAMILIAR*

The body does not work as a series of parts in isolation, but as a whole, dynamically integrated living system. Every cell in the body has receptors for neurotransmitters, so in a real sense, every cell is a nerve cell. We do not see with our eyes or think with our brains, but rather we live in a "minding body." This biological awareness of every cell is really the foundation of vision, the ability to derive meaning and direct action based on patterns of electromagnetic stimuli which we call light.

The skin of the entire body is covered with tiny electric eyes known in Traditional Chinese Medicine (TCM) as acupuncture points. Each is a window of heightened sensitivity of the organism to its energetic environment. What is unique about the acupuncture points compared to the rest of the human skin, our largest organ, is that at these points there is a gathering of blood vessels and nerve cells called a neurovascular bundle.

The most profound window on the world of energy that surrounds us is our eyes themselves. These remarkable sense organs specialize in the transduction of quantum photon energies into electrical nerve signals that account for two thirds of all the nerve current entering the human brain. To accomplish this demands the most concentrated and specialized neurovascular structure in the body. So much is vision dependent on circulation, that the entire blood volume of the body passes through the eyes every 40 minutes or so. Behind the retina lies a tremendous network of blood vessels positioned perfectly to bask in the warmth of natural light.

According to Nobel Laureate, Albert Szent Gyorgi, natural light can stimulate a 400 to 500 percent increase in the performance of not only enzymes and hormones in our blood, but even the basic building blocks like vitamins and minerals. So, not only is vision and eye health dependent on good nutrition, but even our ability to get the most out of our body chemistry depends on the energizing effect of the light entering our eyes. And besides direct energetic effects on the compounds in our blood, there are intricate pathways in the brain that link vision to the regulation of nerve, endocrine and immune functions. This may be one reason why allergies improve in children who develop enhanced visual abilities through vision therapy.

Eye tissue places tremendous demands on all body systems to maintain optimum health and performance, because the process of vision is so exacting. In no other part of the body must the major branches of the nervous system coordinate so closely—a source of tremendous strain under various conditions of stress, whether visual, cognitive, emotional, physical or metabolic. The voluntary nervous system must command the two eyes to position accurately within a tiny fraction of a degree. At the same time this function must maintain precise coordination with focusing which is regulated by the parasympathetic division of the autonomic nervous system. Under mild stress, focusing near gets harder, while converging the two eyes to triangulate the same near target also gets harder. Under moderate stress, focusing gets harder still, and overconvergence produces strain as well on the alignment system. Under severe prolonged stress, the system eventually fatigues, resulting in a general difficulty in both focusing and converging for near visual tasks.

The eyes are unique in many ways, making them a particularly sensitive indicator of our state of well-being. The retina has the highest metabolism of any tissue, thus demanding more oxygen than any other. When breathing is not full and relaxed, for example, when people with visual stress tend to hold their breath when staring to discern visual details, peripheral vision and retinal performance can suffer.

The eyes are like beacons resting atop the tower of the spine and skeletal framework. When the spine is out of alignment, visual centering is necessarily destabilized or at least stressed. And likewise, visual asymmetries and stresses of ocular orientation in space produce adaptive responses through the musculature of the neck, spine and body which result in the tendency to hold chronically warped body postures.

Several teams of chiropractors and behavioral optometrists have found that by applying the two modalities in immediate succession, changes previously thought unattainable, both in vision and in body structure, have become commonplace. While these investigations are not widely disseminated yet, it is common knowledge that much of the enervation affecting vision takes place through the spinal cord. For example, part of the regulation of the pupil passes through the thoracic vertebral segments (mid-back), while the cervical (neck) area supplies sympathetic enervation to the eye area. Similarly, control systems based on light information from the eyes must often pass through the spinal cord to reach their ultimate destinations; for example, the control of the pineal gland, which secretes melatonin in the dark, is regulated by nerve information from the eyes that must pass first through the neck before re-entering the head where the pineal is located.

Obviously, stresses such as subluxations, which can place mechanical stress on these nerve fibers and reduce the flow of information, will have a deleterious effect on this visual function. Also, research at Dartmouth College has shown that the muscles of the neck are directly linked to aniseikonia, a difference in the perceived image size from the two eyes, a visual condition previously thought to be purely optical. Further work by Professor Elliot Forest at the State University of New York, State College of Optometry showed that body posture and related asymmetries in eye movement patterns were directly linked to changes in astigmatism, involving asymmetrical changes in the shape of the eyeball itself.

NUTRITION

And what of nutrition? Certainly the eyes need it and their health is dependent not only on what one eats, but how one digests, absorbs, utilizes and excretes. Heavy metals, pesticides, food additives (e.g., MSG, which has been linked to glaucoma) and other toxins abound in our food, air and water today. Over 70,000 toxic chemicals are now being produced that never existed before in the environment for which our bodies were designed. Americans eat refined food, which has been robbed of the fiber that is essential for proper digestion. As Americans get older, they tend to have weaker and weaker digestive powers and produce fewer enzymes, thus extracting fewer nutrients from their foods.

We need to care for our diet and digestive systems as the lifeline that they are. And this is nowhere more essential than for vision and the eyes. The eyes require one of the highest levels of zinc anywhere in the body. And the highest level of vitamin C and oxygen . . . and on and on. Healthy eyes demand a healthy body.

The eyes are in fact the windows to changes happening elsewhere in the body. High blood pressure and diabetes are just two conditions that effect changes in the eyes; others include impurities in the bloodstream, hardening of the arteries, stagnation in the liver, problems with digestion and elimination and poor circulation. All of these things, along with other bodily imbalances form the basis of eye disease. It is important to remember that the health of the eyes cannot be better than the state of the vital organs of the body.

Ill health anywhere in the body clearly shows up in the eyes—not once but twice. It is mapped on the iris, independently discovered by two physicians in different parts of Europe, and it is mapped in the white of the eye, an observation first made by Native Americans. Modern energetic medicine is further mapping relationships between the various parts of the eye and the rest of the body, as does Traditional Chinese Medicine. In Chinese medicine, the five elements and the organs relating to them correspond to the eyes in the following manner:

Organ	Corresponding Eye Parts
Liver	Cornea, iris
Kidneys	Pupil, aqueous humor, lens, vitreous, retina, optic nerves, choroid

Spleen	Upper eyelids, lachrymal ducts
Stomach	Lower eyelids
Lungs	Sclera, conjunctivia
Heart	Corners of the eyes

The more we learn of the body's natural interconnectedness, the more we realize that interconnectedness is the essence of the body and how it works. It is not some quirky side effect of a random evolution, but the infinitely intricate weaving of an intelligence great enough to create life itself.

WATER

Another factor that is as important as nutrition but perhaps even more often overlooked, is water. First of all, we need enough of it. Eight eight-ounce glasses a day is often recommended. But in actuality, our bloodstream can only handle being diluted by about four ounces at any one time, so any additional will go immediately to the kidneys to be filtered out to maintain the osmotic balance of the blood. This means more work for the kidneys to filter water that hasn't even had the chance to filter through the lymph system and clean the body's tissues. This process takes about a half hour, so actually we should drink 16 four-ounce glasses of water a day, on a half-hourly schedule. After about three days on such a schedule, even your kidneys will start to adapt and function more efficiently than before.

Is all water the same? Emphatically not. In studies of the relationship of water to health, it's been found that it is the energy balance of the water that most influenced health and disease. This is determined largely by two factors: the pH (acid-alkaline balance) and the ORP (oxidation-reduction potential). The pH actually measures protons, the body's smallest positive ion (electrically charged particle). The ORP is a measure of electrons, the smallest negatively charged ion. For rejuvenating effects to reverse the ravages of aging and disease, we need to drink water that is low in protons, but rich in electrons. Such water acts, in itself, as an antioxidant. And since the human body is made up of about 70 percent water (the blood is 90 percent water), this is a powerful force against the attack of free radicals associated with processes of inflammation and degeneration, such as in glaucoma, macular degeneration, cataracts and even pink eye and dry eye syndromes.

In fact, every disease is now believed to ultimately do its damage by way of these free radicals, which like little fires in our cells, can be quenched by electron donors called antioxidants. Free radicals are often caused by an excess of toxins or even metabolic wastes, which are typically acid (high in protons). When the water of the body is alkaline (low in protons), this provides more room for wastes before they build up to damaging levels.

Two types of water treatment are available today that meet these criteria for a truly healing water. They are Alkamine Coral Calcium water and Alkaline Microwater (contact the Remission Foundation; see Resources). Microwater technology produces a high-tech healing water, which is actually able to penetrate into body tissues, cells and lymph channels, about ten times better than regular water. This is extremely beneficial in bringing needed nutrition to the cells, and also in carrying away wastes, which is particularly critical in hard-to-reach areas that lack direct circulation, like the joints and the lens of the eye. These waters are also crucial in problems related to circulation like diabetes, hypertension, glaucoma and macular degeneration.

THE ROLE OF THE THYROID IN EYE HEALTH

One of the relationships that has been found to be particularly important to vision is that of the thyroid gland in regulating the body's basal energy metabolism. When thyroid function is low, the liver does not have enough energy to break beta-carotene down into vitamin A, a process necessary to support night vision, comfortable adaptation to bright lights, a comfortable moisturizing ability on the front surface of the eyes and sometimes even daytime focusing of the eyes. Hypothyroidism is also associated with macular degeneration, diabetic retinopathy and low-pressure glaucoma.

If you are hypothyroid, consume foods that are naturally high in iodine, such as fish, kelp and root vegetables such as potatoes. Avoid foods that naturally slow down the functioning of the thyroid such as Brussels sprouts, mustard greens, broccoli, turnips, kale and other members of the cabbage family. Avoid sulfa drugs and antihistamines, which aggravate this problem. If you are on thyroid medication, increase calcium supplementation. Also increase daily consumption of foods high in vitamin B complex, such as whole grains, raw nuts and seeds.

Since the thyroid regulates the basal metabolic rate, one way to check for this is to measure body temperature first thing on waking in the morning before even sitting up in bed or opening your eyes (your brain temperature immediately rises several degrees when you open your eyes in the morning). If your temperature is low (below 97.8°F.) talk to your health practitioner about taking a thyroid glandular supplement in addition to iodine, copper and zinc, as well as supplementing with preformed vitamin A and beta-carotene.

Zinc is also needed for proper vitamin A metabolism which affects night vision, wound healing, dry eye symptoms, immunity and many other functions. Zinc also affects glandular function, such as thyroid activity. Check your zinc level with a zinc taste test. Eighty-five percent of people with low zinc levels can raise them to normal in four weeks. The other 15 percent usually have parasite problems that need to be cleared first.

The bottom line is that checking both basal metabolism and zinc status are important pieces of the puzzle in understanding and correcting eye health imbalances. The following chapter explores more fully the role that nutrition plays in eye health and how TCM, herbal and homeopathic remedies and eye exercises can help.

CHAPTER 1

Seeing Better Naturally: Treating Eye Disorders Holistically

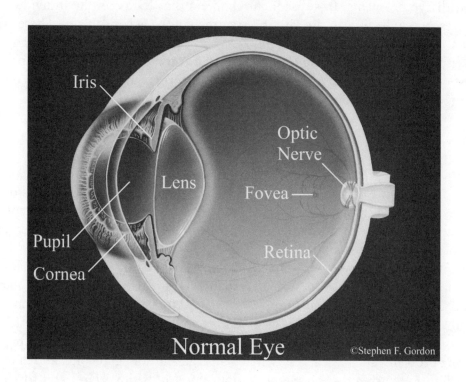

Iris

Optic Nerve

Lens

Fovea

Pupil

Cornea

Retina

Normal Eye ©Stephen F. Gordon

Medical science doesn't really know why or how most poor eyesight develops, yet it wrongly believes that eyesight almost always worsens, that it rarely improves by itself, and that once eyesight starts to go, nothing can be done about it; all we can do is stand idly by as it deteriorates. The good news is that we don't have to be passive victims of eye disease. Eye deterioration can often be stopped — and even reversed. Throughout this book, we're going to tell you how.

Holistically, you are more than an interesting set of symptoms that must be eradicated with the proper drug. You are a complex human being functioning on several levels: mental, emotional, spiritual and physical. In holistic medicine, we take all of these levels into consideration when we treat a patient, because we believe that merely quelling the physical symptoms of disease doesn't address how that disease impacts and emerges from all of those other levels of your being.

In this chapter, we will discuss the various treatments we use in helping people with eye problems. In subsequent chapters that focus on the individual eye diseases, we will discuss the specific treatment for each problem. These treatments — nutrition, Traditional Chinese Medicine, acupressure, herbs, physical exercise, eye exercises, spinal adjustments and homeopathy — each support a holistic way of viewing eye problems and offer natural methods of balancing the multifaceted cause of disease.

NUTRITION

When Mom and Dad told you to eat your carrots because they were good for your eyes, they were on the right track. As researchers continue to document that we really are what we eat, the role of nutrition in eye health becomes clearer — and more important — all the time.

Consider these facts: More than 25 percent of the nutrients we absorb from our food go to nourish our "visual system" — our eyes and all of the nerves, blood vessels and tissues that support our vision. Indeed, the concentration of vitamin C in healthy eyes is higher than almost anywhere else in the body.[1] It's not surprising, then, that proper nutrition plays an important role in preventing and treating problems such as cataracts, macular degeneration, glaucoma and dry eyes.

What do we mean when we talk about good nutrition? First and foremost, we mean balance; it is essential to eat a variety of whole foods. The body does not use each vitamin and mineral in isolation. The absence of one nutrient can affect the body's ability to use another. For example, proper amounts of magnesium and vitamin D are needed to absorb and utilize calcium efficiently. Without adequate levels of zinc, the body cannot utilize all of the vitamin A it receives. Similarly, the B vitamins are needed together, working properly only as a team.

Eating a variety of whole foods and omitting sweets and other junk foods will help ensure that you're getting a wide range of nutrients. The body can lose a significant amount of nutrients when we eat nutrient-poor foods. For example, we lose chromium and B vitamins as our body tries to burn white sugar. Caffeine, medications and preservatives also deplete the vitamins and minerals that are needed for healthy eyes and good vision.

Yet, in today's world, it is probably not realistic to expect to get all of our nutrients from food alone. No matter how wholesome and pure our food might be, there are other factors that affect its nutrient content: how it is grown, how it is stored and how it is cooked all affect nutrient levels. Besides, science determines the nutrient value of food under ideal laboratory conditions. What your body actually absorbs can be very different. Your age, health, activity and stress levels also can affect what your body needs and how well it's using the nutrients from your diet. For example, both aging and reduced liver health are associated with increasing eye problems because they reduce the absorption and utilization of key nutrients from food.

This is where supplements come in handy. And it's likely that you will need more than the Recommended Dietary Allowances set by the government for healthy people. We routinely recommend vitamin and mineral supplements to our patients, but simply taking vitamin pills and ignoring the benefits of good food isn't the answer either.

The Vision Diet

Throughout this book, we will discuss in depth the role of nutrition in six common eye problems: cataracts, glaucoma, macular degeneration, floaters, sties and conjunctivitis. Although each problem has its own particular nutrition requirements, let's set some general guidelines. First, eliminate foods on the outside of the food target (see p. 12) and emphasize foods toward the center.

The diet we recommend for the treatment of eye disease is one that maintains a healthy balance of body chemistry. See the following guidelines from nutritional biochemist Jay D. Foster.[2]

Dr. Swartwout's Food Target
Set Your Sights on a Healthy Diet

Carbohydrates
regeneration

Fats & Oils
energy regulation

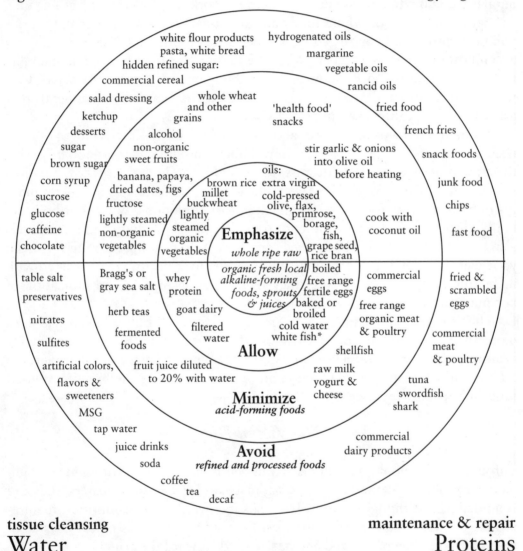

white flour products
pasta, white bread
hidden refined sugar:
commercial cereal
salad dressing
ketchup
desserts
sugar
brown sugar
corn syrup
sucrose
glucose
caffeine
chocolate

hydrogenated oils
margarine
vegetable oils
rancid oils
fried food
french fries
snack foods
junk food
chips
fast food

whole wheat
and other
grains
alcohol
non-organic
sweet fruits
banana, papaya,
dried dates, figs
fructose
lightly steamed
non-organic
vegetables

'health food'
snacks

stir garlic & onions
into olive oil
before heating

brown rice
millet
buckwheat
lightly
steamed
organic
vegetables

oils:
extra virgin
cold-pressed
olive, flax,
primrose,
borage,
fish,
grape seed,
rice bran

cook with
coconut oil

Emphasize
whole ripe raw

*organic fresh local
alkaline-forming
foods, sprouts
& juices*

table salt
preservatives
nitrates
sulfites
artificial colors,
flavors &
sweeteners
MSG
tap water
juice drinks
soda
coffee
tea
decaf

Bragg's or
gray sea salt
herb teas
fermented
foods
fruit juice diluted
to 20% with water

whey
protein
goat dairy
filtered
water

boiled
free range
fertile eggs
baked or
broiled
cold water
white fish*

commercial
eggs
free range
organic meat
& poultry

fried &
scrambled
eggs

commercial
meat
& poultry

shellfish
raw milk
yogurt &
cheese

tuna
swordfish
shark

Allow

Minimize
acid-forming foods

Avoid
refined and processed foods

commercial
dairy products

tissue cleansing
Water

maintenance & repair
Proteins

*Allowed fish include: cod, flounder, haddock, halibut, herring, mackerel, Pacific salmon, perch, pollock, rockfish, sardine, scrod, sole

Note: The foods that have been eliminated or restricted on this diet have been shown to upset body chemistry and therefore prevent effective balancing of that chemistry with the nutritional supplements that have been recommended for you. In order to achieve the best chemical balance possible, we urge you to follow this diet as closely as possible.

THE VISION DIET

Foods to Enjoy:

Vegetables All are allowed; raw or steamed are best. Frozen are the next best to fresh vegetables if they have no sauce, sugar or other additives. Potatoes are very good, but be sure to include the skin. Sprouts are good additions to salads. Olive oil, other cold-pressed oils, and a good vinegar (i.e., balsamic) or other natural salad dressing may be used.

Eggs Eggs are recommended, with organic the healthiest choice. Soft boiled or poached give the greatest nutritional value.

Butter We recommend unsalted, real butter. Avoid margarine.

Meats All lean meats, poultry and fish are permitted, including shellfish. Most experts agree that red meat should be limited to about once per week or so. Pork should be mostly avoided. It is best to remove the skin of poultry since most hormones and antibiotics collect there. Remember to cook your chicken well.

Snacks Nuts, seeds, popcorn, rice cakes, whole grain crackers with tuna, egg or tofu salad; almond or other nut butters; raw vegetables with hummus or other bean dip.

Seasonings All natural herbs and spices may be used. Sea salt is better in small amounts than regular table salt. Also try Herbamare, Seazun or kelp.

Grains Always use whole grains: brown rice, whole wheat, rye, millet, buckwheat, oats, etc. Avoid breads with hydrogenated oils or corn sweeteners. Oatmeal and oat bran make excellent hot cereals.

Water Avoid regular tap water. Distilled water from a stainless-steel distiller is the best. Soft plastic containers should be avoided; use hard plastic or glass containers. Bottled mineral waters or sparkling waters are much better than tap water. Drink 6–8 8 oz. glasses daily.

Fruits Eat 1–2 pieces per day maximum if you tend to have a sugar intolerance or hypoglycemic reaction. Apples, melons, berries and bananas are the best fruits to choose from. Fruits should not be eaten alone for blood sugar stability, but with nuts, a small snack or with a meal. Small amounts of diluted apple juice are often tolerated in moderation. Fresh, natural vegetable juices are usually well tolerated.

Foods to Avoid:

Caffeine Coffee, colas, regular tea and any herb containing caffeine.

Sugar White, brown, turbinado, cane, raw, sugar substitutes, candy, pastries, ice cream and any other foods that contain excessive sugar. Also read labels to avoid dextrose, lactose, glucose, maltose and any other *-ose* ingredient. Honey can usually be tolerated in small amounts.

Dairy Milk, cheese, yogurt, ice cream. Butter is the only product from cows that is acceptable. Milk and cheese from goats and sheep can be used. Or use soy milk instead.

White Flour Avoid (use whole wheat or other whole grain flours).

Alcohol Avoid or have one drink no more than 1–2 times per week.

Condiments Avoid products containing artificial colors, flavors or preservatives. Avoid table salt, MSG (monosodium glutamate), Accent, or any product with hydrogenated oils or sweeteners.

VITAMINS AND MINERALS

In addition to eating well, there are certain vitamin and mineral supplements that are essential for your visual health. While specific recommendations for each condition are mentioned in the corresponding chapters, the following is more indepth information on the essential fatty acids and L-Glutathione, which are utilized in most of the eye conditions discussed in the book.

Essential Fatty Acids

Essential fatty acids, also called EFAs, are just as essential to a healthy balance of body chemistry, and thus proper cell function as good food, vitamins and minerals. They are an integral component of nerve cells, cell membranes and vital hormone-like substances known as prostaglandins, which help to regulate numerous body functions, including normal immune response during inflammation. These unsaturated fatty acids are also necessary for healthy skin, hair and nails; have a supportive effect on the circulatory system; and can reduce blood cholesterol levels.

Unfortunately, diets typically consumed in the United States and other developed countries do not provide sufficient amounts of the richest sources of these beneficial essential fatty acids. Our consumption of saturated fats from meat and dairy foods is often too high, while our intake of unsaturated fats from fish and certain vegetable oil sources is often too low. In addition, modern food processing techniques frequently remove or alter the levels of important fatty acids, so adding these EFAs back into the diet with certain foods or supplements is advised.

There are two basic types of EFAs: omega-3 and omega-6. The best sources of omega-3 EFAs are the flesh of cold water marine fish (salmon, herring, mackerel) as well as black currant seed oil, flaxseed and flaxseed oil and hemp seed. Omega-6 EFAs are found in evening primrose oil, borage oil and black currant seed oil. In general, we recommend 1,500 mg per day of the essential fatty acids.

L-Glutathione

Since the 1900s glutathione has been shown to be essential for eye health. Low glutathione levels have been linked to cataracts, macular degeneration, glaucoma and floaters. Glutathione is considered by many to be the most important antioxidant made by the body and is integrally involved in maintaining good vision. Glutathione is composed of three amino acids: cysteine, glycine and glutamic acid. The eye nutrients that can help increase glutathione levels are: N-acetyl-cysteine (NAC), alpha lipoic acid, vitamin C, vitamin B2, vitamin B6, selenium and zinc. Melatonin, pycnogenol and grapeseed extract can also boost glutathione levels.

N-acetyl-cysteine is a valuable nutrient used by the body for glutathione synthesis inside cells. It also has antioxidant properties of its own. Alpha lipoic acid enhances the movement of blood sugar into the cells, thereby maintaining balanced blood sugar metabolism. Selenium is an antioxidant which helps fight free radical damage while increasing the potency of vitamin E; zinc is necessary for protein synthesis and amino acid production. Both are necessary for optimal production of glutathione.

VITAMINS AND MINERALS FOR VISUAL HEALTH

The following are the vitamins and minerals that are important to maintain good visual functioning. In the following chapters, specific recommendations and dosages will be given for specific eye conditions.

Nutritional Supplements	*Dosages*
Vitamin A	10,000 I.U.
Beta-carotene	15,000 I.U.
Vitamin B1 (thiamine)	50 mg
Vitamin B2 (riboflavin)	50 mg
Vitamin B3 (niacin)	50 mg
Vitamin B5 (pantothenic acid)	400 mg
Vitamin B6 (pyridoxine)	50 mg
Vitamin B12	100 mcg
Folic acid	800 mcg
Biotin	300 mcg
Choline	150 mcg
Inositol	50 mg
PABA (para-amino benzoic acid)	50 mg
Vitamin E (d-alpha tocopheryl succinate)	400 I.U.
Vitamin D	100 I.U.
Vitamin K (phytonadione)	60 mcg
Calcium	500 mg for men, 800 mg for women
Magnesium	500 mg
Potassium	100 mg
Copper	2 mg
Manganese	20 mg
Zinc	20 mg
Iodine (Kelp)	150 mcg
Chromium	200 mcg
Selenium	200 mcg
Molybdenum	150 mcg
Vanadium	200 mcg
N-acetyl-cysteine	500 mg

Taurine	500 mg
Lutein	6 mg
Zeaxanthin	300 mcg
Omega-3 fatty acids	500 mg
Omega-6 fatty acids	500 mg
Bioflavonoids	100 mg

TRADITIONAL CHINESE MEDICINE (TCM)

The human body is an organic unit with its tissues and organs interrelated and mutually dependent. Therefore, the health of the eyes, being the optical organ of the body, can influence — and be influenced by — any and every other organ in the body. Makes sense, right? Not to everyone. Particularly not to Western medicine. But to practitioners of Traditional Chinese Medicine (TCM), dealing with the body holistically is the basis of their practice. A TCM practitioner is trained to put the body's energy back into balance by using herbs, acupuncture, acupressure and other methods.

The Five Elements

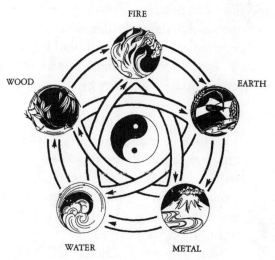

Thousands of years ago, Chinese philosophers created the Wu Hsing or Five Element System to explain how the primary forces of nature ebb and flow within the human body. Each of the five elements — wood, water, earth, metal and fire — depends upon the others, and life depends upon their intricate balance and interdependence. In Chinese medicine, the emphasis is on patterns of body function in contrast to the Western structural bias.

Reprinted with permission from *Feminine Healing* by Jason Elias and Katherine Ketcham. New York: Warner Books, 1995.

Thus, while Western terms corresponding to organs are used, they refer here to functional processes which often represent the organ that characterizes them.

The Chinese believe that both physical and emotional dysfunctions are due to an imbalance in these energies. Therefore, all eye conditions can be viewed as either an excess or deficiency in certain elemental energies.

The Wood Element. Glaucoma can be looked at as "excess wood," which means that the wood element's energy is out of balance and in excess and therefore is creating high pressure in the eye. The liver and gall bladder are the organs associated with wood, and the liver is the organ most directly related to eye health; your visual ability depends on how well the liver does its job. The liver metabolizes carbohydrates, fats and proteins, providing important nourishment essential for the eyes. In TCM, it is the most important organ for storing blood and by doing so, it regulates the volume of blood in the body at any given time.

The liver also controls the state of the tendons, which affects our capacity for movement and physical activity. The tendon's capacity for contraction and relaxation—so important in the eye — depends on the nourishment and circulation of the blood from the liver.

In TCM, the liver also is the organ responsible for regulating and dispersing the flow of energy — called *qi* (pronounced "chee") — throughout the body. When qi is unbalanced, illness occurs.

Unbalanced qi in the gall bladder, which stores the bile manufactured by the liver, is associated with glaucoma as well as conjunctivitis, light sensitivity (photophobia), floaters and dry eyes.

> The liver stores the blood. During the day, the liver provides the blood for movement and activities so that the blood can circulate through the channels and collaterals. At night, when one sleeps, the blood returns to the liver. When the liver is nourished by the blood, one can see. When the feet are perfused with blood, one can walk. When the hands are nourished by blood, they can grasp. When the fingers are provided with blood, one can carry.
> — THE YELLOW EMPEROR'S CLASSIC OF INTERNAL MEDICINE
> BY HUANG DI

The Fire Element. The four organ systems associated with fire are the heart and its lining, the *pericardium,* the small intestine and the triple heater. The triple heater (what Western medicine calls the endocrine system) is responsible for heating and cooling the entire body. When the triple heater is not working in harmony with the body, excess heat in the upper part of the body can result in glaucoma, conjunctivitis, sties or dry eyes.

As important as the liver is in regulating the qi, the heart has an equally profound job: In Traditional Chinese Medicine, the heart is in charge of blood flow throughout the body. Heart "energy" is what causes blood to course through the blood vessels. Any heart dysfunction will decrease the amount of blood flow, resulting in a lack of nourishment to the eye. This lack of nourishment, of course, results in disease.

The small intestine is considered part of this blood nourishment system because it is there that food is broken down into usable nutrients and those that must be excreted. The small intestine absorbs the usable nutrients and carries them to the spleen, where they are transformed into qi and blood. If the heart, small intestine and spleen are doing their jobs, your eyes will be moist and clear. If they're not, you can expect symptoms which may include conjunctivitis, light sensitivity, excess tearing and dry eyes.

The Water Element. Remember that in Traditional Chinese Medicine, all organs are interrelated; they influence and are influenced by every other organ. Let's look at the role of the kidneys. The kidneys receive and store the essences of *all* of the other organs. (In Chinese medicine, essence is the original material that forms the basis of all other tissues; in Western medicine, we would call it DNA.) Since visual function depends on nourishment from the essence of all of the other organs, there is a close relationship between the health of the kidneys and the health of the eyes.

Of course the kidneys have another job too — that of controlling water metabolism in the body. The kidneys and the bladder are the main organs associated with the water element. The kidneys play an important role in the distribution, retention and excretion of water. The bladder stores and excretes water, so it too is part of this system. When this system is working up to par and the kidney essence or qi is flowing throughout the body the way it should, water and other body fluids will be transformed into tears and aqueous humor, and your eyes will be clear and bright. Cataracts, macular degeneration, dry eyes and conjunctivitis are all associated with the dysfunction of the kidneys and bladder. The water element has a special link to the aqueous humor and the pupil.

The Earth Element. The spleen, an earth element, is responsible for transporting nutrients and qi throughout the body, particularly upward; the stomach, the other earth element, sends them downward. When they're functioning normally, the eyes are nourished. As the muscles of the eyes obtain nutrients, the eyeballs can move freely and the eyelids open and close easily. If you're having stomach trouble, or if your spleen isn't doing its job, you may be prone to such eye problems as conjunctivitis, sties, retinal edema, macular degeneration, blepharitis and other eyelid disorders.

The Metal Element. In Chinese medicine, there is a belief that the metal organs — the lungs and large intestine — instinctively know when to let substances in and when to let them go. In its function as the oxygen metabolizer, the lungs oversee the ongoing interaction between the inner and outer worlds, inhaling oxygen and exhaling carbon dioxide. They are in charge of dispersing and distributing qi, blood and body fluids to the eyes. The lungs also conduct fluid downward to the bladder, so they also serve as body purifiers. When these dispersing functions are normal, blood circulates freely to warm and nourish the eyes.

According to Traditional Chinese Medicine, the lungs work in tandem with the large intestine. The large intestine is continuously discriminating between substances the body can use and those it cannot, between harmless elements and harmful ones. If there's a problem in the large intestine, lung energy can't descend there, and the eye problems that can result include conjunctivitis, light sensitivity (photophobia), macular degeneration and blue sclera, in which the whites of the eyes turn blue. The metal element is also linked to the vitreous humor and floaters.

ACUPRESSURE

Acupuncture is the ancient Chinese medical practice of inserting needles into the skin at certain points of the body to improve, rebalance or redirect qi. Acupressure is similar to acupuncture, except that pressure rather than needles is applied to those points. This pressure, applied by the hands, releases muscular tension and promotes the circulation of blood and qi to aid healing.

The studies that support acupuncture and acupressure as successful healing arts are recent, but these treatments are more than 5,000 years old. The Chinese discovered that pressing certain points on the body relieved pain and also benefited other parts of the body more remote from the pain and the pressure points. Gradually they learned that the treatment also influenced the function of the internal organs.

In early Chinese dynasties, when stones and arrows were the implements of war, many soldiers wounded on the battlefield reported that diseases or conditions that had plagued them for years had suddenly vanished. Naturally, such strange occurrences baffled the physicians who could find no logical relationship between the trauma and the ensuing recovery. But after years of meticulous observation, ancient Chinese physicians learned they could cure certain illnesses by striking or piercing specific places on the skin.[3]

But how does it work? Chinese physicians conceived of the points as junctures of special pathways, called *meridians,* that carry the human energy called qi. These junctures are especially sensitive to bioelectric impulses in the body. When pressure or needles are applied to those points, those impulses are readily conducted throughout the body.

Using modern, sophisticated equipment, Western researchers have confirmed how this works: Specifically stimulating these points triggers electrical changes in various parts of the body, as well as the release of *endorphins,* neurochemicals that relieve pain. As a result of the stimulation, the flow of blood and oxygen to the affected area is also increased. This causes the muscles to relax and promotes healing.

Besides relieving pain, acupressure and acupuncture can rebalance qi throughout the body, helping the immune system fight off invaders and dissolving the tension and stress that can keep you from functioning smoothly.

We've found acupressure to be very beneficial in the treatment of eye disease, and we recommend it in this book because it is easy, doesn't cost anything and you can do it yourself. For a full explanation of how to perform acupressure on your specific eye problem, consult the acupressure section at the end of the chapter that discusses your particular eye problem. Note which pressure points should be massaged, then turn to the Appendix on pages 131–38 for the location of those points and for specific instructions on how to massage them and how often. You'll know you've located the correct point when you slide your fingers along the general area until they rest naturally in a depression or hollow which tends to be slightly more sensitive than the surrounding area. When an imbalance or disharmony of energies exists, the acupuncture point tends to be sensitive, sometimes even painful, to the touch.

HERBAL REMEDIES

Long before there were drug companies and pharmacies, people used herbs for medicinal purposes.[4] Modern researchers are now confirming that herbs have an enormous and exciting range of healing powers, and that they can be a safe, natural, accessible and inexpensive alternative to synthetic drugs. Plus, when prescribed properly, they have few, if any, side effects.

Up until the 20th century, most medicines prescribed in this country were herbal remedies, prepared from the roots, leaves and flowers of plants. When wonder drugs, such as penicillin, were developed in the 1920s, the popularity of herbal remedies began to wane. Modern medicine co-opted their use, and now, 25 percent of modern prescription and over-the-counter drugs are derived from herbs.

In other countries, herbal remedies have never lost their popular nor professional appeal. Scientists in Europe, China and Japan routinely research herbs. In Europe, for example, herbs are sold side-by-side on pharmacy shelves with conventional pharmaceutical drugs, and doctors are as likely to recommend an herbal remedy as they are a prescription drug.

Herbal remedies are making a comeback in this country, however, and one reason is the way herbs work. Many conventional medicines are designed to cure symptoms of a disease rather than correct the underlying causes of the disease itself. Some herbal treatments work a lot like conventional medicines, but others enable the body to activate its resources to neutralize chemical and biological stresses, which herbalists refer to as the underlying toxic state that is causing the symptoms. Most herbalists see the standard medical practice of suppressing symptoms as an interruption of the body's natural healing processes. Remember when a fever was to be broken at all costs? These days we're told that fevers help fight the disease.

Herbal medicine is another treatment modality that takes a holistic approach to healing, viewing the patient as a whole rather than a body part, and remembering that illness in one part of the body could very well be affecting another part.

We recommend that you take herbs in the form of tinctures or extracts; be sure to follow the directions for each remedy carefully.

Sometimes people prefer pills or capsules to avoid the bitter taste of an herb, but we usually don't recommend pills or capsules since the active constituents of the herb aren't as readily available to the body in a pill or capsule as they are in a tincture, extract or tea. Plus, the taste stimulation is an important part of taking herbs. The bitterness provokes a series of bodily actions important to the healing process, such as stimulating bile flow and other digestive juices and regulating insulin and other hormones. Of course, pills and capsules are convenient when you can't take time for herbal tea or when you're traveling.

For external eye conditions, such as conjunctivitis or sties, you can also apply a compress of the recommended herb two or three times a day while also taking it internally. To make a compress, add one or two teaspoons of the herbal tincture to a cup of boiling water, or use an herbal tea (see below). Let it cool slightly. Dampen a clean washcloth with the herbal tea and place it on the affected area for three minutes.

How to Make an Herbal Tincture or Tea

A tincture is made by steeping one ounce of dried or three ounces of fresh herbs in five ounces of alcohol. Tinctures are available through herbalists or in most health food stores. However, if you prefer to make your own tinctures, steep the herbs in 100 proof vodka in a small, sterile, airtight bottle. Let it sit for two to six weeks (shake it vigorously about once a week) so that the active components of the herb can be fully released into the alcohol. If you prefer, or if you are sensitive to alcohol, use apple cider vinegar instead of vodka. Strain out the herbs and bottle. To take a tincture, add the recommended dosage to a cup of warm water to make a tea. (This will cause most of the alcohol to evaporate and dilute any bitterness.) An herbal tea can also be made by steeping 1 teaspoon dried or 1 tablespoon of fresh herbs in one cup of boiling water for 10 minutes.

HOMEOPATHIC REMEDIES

Homeopathy is based on a fundamental principle called "like cures like." In other words, a substance that can cause symptoms in large amounts can cure similar conditions in minute amounts. Homeopathy works a lot like a vaccination: tiny amounts of these substances stimulate your immune system to help the body heal itself. Because the eyes are delicate and sensitive, eye conditions are particularly receptive to homeopathic treatments.

Homeopathic remedies are effective, safe and have no side effects. But they react differently from conventional medications because of the way they are formulated. Homeopathic medicines are activated by being diluted and vigorously shaken. Although no one quite understands how homeopathy works, we do know that the more dilute the remedy is and the more it is activated, the more potent it is.

In addition, homeopathic remedies are more individualized than conventional medicines. For example, if you have a cold with a fever and a sore throat that was relieved by a warm drink, you'd receive a different homeopathic remedy than someone else with the same illness, but who found cool drinks soothing. Homeopaths interview their patients at length to find just the right remedy for that individual's personality and symptoms.

Throughout this book, we recommend several homeopathic remedies for different eye conditions. However, for a more individualized treatment, we recommend that you see a qualified homeopathic practitioner.

PHYSICAL EXERCISE

Aerobic exercise not only benefits your heart. It's good for your eyes too.

Exercise is extremely important in the prevention of chronic eye diseases. Exercise raises oxygen levels in the cells and increases lymph and blood circulation. This increased circulation is a prerequisite to good visual health, because it revitalizes the organs and glands and speeds up detoxification of the body.

We recommend that you gently build up to aerobic exercise for a minimum of 20 minutes per day, four days a week. You don't have to join a health club or run five miles a day or benchpress 300 pounds to have good vision. Here's what we recommend:

1. *Rebounding.* A rebounder is a mini-trampoline. Rebounding — gentle jumping on the trampoline — keeps blood flowing and improves circulation, particularly in the legs and head. To begin the exercise, stand flat-footed on the rebounder mat. Gently swing your arms a few times and then begin bouncing. Gentle bouncing will do; you don't have to jump up and down with terrific force to gain the benefits of rebounding.

2. *Walking or jogging.* Get a good, comfortable, supportive pair of walking or jogging shoes, and select a route that won't have you pounding concrete (it's bad for your joints).

3. *Exercise bicycle, Stairmaster, or NordicTrack.* You might have to go to a gym for a Stairmaster, but inexpensive used exercise bicycles are widely available in the classified ads of your daily newspaper.

Because aerobic exercise also generates free radicals, it is extremely important that you also take a good antioxidant supplement.

EYE EXERCISES

Everyone knows that you have to exercise muscles to keep them fit. This applies not only to your heart, leg and arm muscles, but to your eye muscles as well. To improve visual fitness, you need to regularly exercise your eye muscles.

There are six exercises that should be part of your overall visual health program.

1. **Palming.** The palming exercise will teach you to relax your eyes, which in turn will bring healthy energy to your eyes.

    First, rub your hands together until they feel warm (about 15 to 20 seconds). Then place your cupped hands over your closed eyes, being careful not to touch your eyes with the palms of your hands. The fingers of each hand should overlap and rest gently on the center of your forehead. Don't create any unnecessary pressure on your face. If your arms get tired, rest your elbows on a table.

Sit quietly for one to two minutes with your hands over your eyes. The more relaxed you become, the blacker the darkness you will see with your eyes closed.

Palming

2. **Sunning.** Just what it implies, this relaxing exercise nourishes the visual system. Close your eyes and face the sun. Do not tighten your facial muscles. Let the sun shine on your closed eyes for five seconds. Then place your palm over your closed eyes for five seconds. Remove your hand, and let the sun shine on your closed eyes for five more seconds. Repeat 10 times.

Sunning

3. **Scanning.** This exercise helps you increase the flexibility of your eyes. Standing at one end of a room, let your eyes scan around the edges of objects in the room — clocks, television sets, doors, lights, computers, etc. The object of

this exercise is to keep your eyes moving in a loose and fluid way. Do this exercise for three to five minutes a day, remembering to breathe.

4. **Near-far focus.** This exercise also improves eye flexibility.

Hold your thumb six inches from your nose. Focus on your thumb. Take one deep breath and exhale slowly. Then focus on an object about 10 feet away. Take another deep breath and slowly exhale. Repeat 15 times per day.

5. **Chinese massage.** More than a thousand years ago, the Chinese already had created many forms of therapeutic treatment. One, called *Tui-Na* or pushing-pulling massage, isn't exactly massage as we know it, but rather provides pressure to certain points on the face to stimulate the muscles around the eyes, the blood vessels, nerve endings and the acupuncture points in this area.

Three parts of the hand are used: the palms, the thumb pads and the pads of the index fingers. (Always use the pads of the thumbs and index fingers or your fingernails might scratch your face.) Pressure is always steady, even, and gentle; never press harder than is comfortable, and release the pressure slowly. Do not massage or rub the skin. Stay focused and concentrate on what you're doing. (It will actually help increase the blood flow to the eye muscles.)

Once or twice a day, do the following:

A. Sit quietly in a chair with your eyes closed and take eight to ten deep breaths. Feel the air flowing in and out of your lungs.

B. Press your palms together firmly and rub them rapidly until they feel very warm. Cover your closed eyes with your warmed palms. Sit quietly and feel the warmth penetrate the area around your eyes. Take five deep breaths.

C. With the pads of your thumb and index finger, press inward and firmly squeeze the bridge of your nose while you take ten deep breaths with your eyes closed.

D. With the pads of your thumbs, apply pressure upward between your eyebrows for 10 to 15 seconds. Keep your eyes closed.

E. With the pads of your index fingers, press at the bottom edge of the bony eye socket (called the *inferior border of the orbit*) for ten seconds with your eyes closed.

Chinese Massage

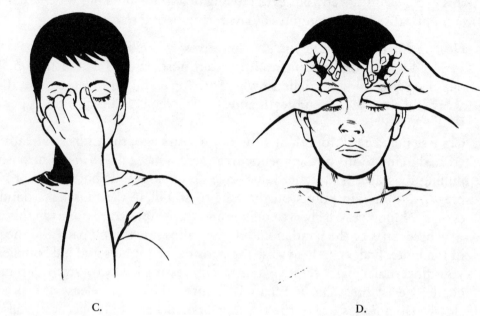

C.   D.

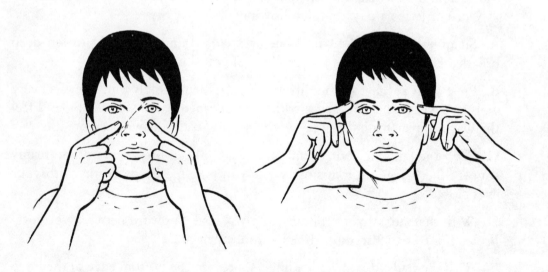

E.   F.

F. With the pads of your thumbs, press gently but firmly at a point about one millimeter from the outer edge of the eye orbit. Keep eyes closed.

6. **Eye Stretch.** This exercise develops freedom of movement in the connective tissues around your eyes.

A. Stand in a relaxed posture, look straight ahead with both eyes open.

B. Place the sides of your index fingers against the skin to the right of each eye. Look to the left as you stretch the skin and connective tissues around your eyes to the right. Inhale as you look to the left, and exhale as you look back to the center.

C. Repeat with your index fingers to the left of each eye, looking to the right as you stretch the skin to the right.

D. Now stretch the skin downward with your fingers while looking upward.

E. Now stretch the skin below your eyebrows upward with the sides of your index fingers.

F. Repeat the sequence six times, taking a longer, deeper breath each time. Sustain each stretch through one or more breath cycles, working your way up to six breath cycles in each of the four stretch directions.

Can you feel the release of tension around your eyes? Which eye has more stress stored in the surrounding tissues? In which direction do you get more release of stress and tension? What happens if you sustain a stretch in each direction while breathing in and out? Can you visualize the oxygen from each breath circulating into the area you are stretching?

Ask yourself these questions after each exercise session. What was hard, easy or different than before, and what did you learn about your eyes?

SPINAL ADJUSTMENT

In our practice, we have found that patients with vision problems greatly improve when spinal adjustment is added to the therapy. Whether it be chiropractic, osteopathy, cranial-sacral or spinal manipulation, the therapy ensures that the spinal cord is free from muscular contraction, tension and mechanical nerve pressure, perhaps from a dislocated vertebrae. Any of these problems can interfere with tissue nourishment and adequate nerve flow which the eyes need to function and especially to heal.

It is especially important to pay attention to the upper cervical and midthoracic vertebrae, which supply the eyes with the nerve flow needed for vision and eye function. We have found that adding spinal readjustment therapy often helps enhance the healing process.

EMOTIONAL HEALTH

Most holistic physicians these days believe in an emotional basis for illness. Emotions can cause the release of chemicals in our brains that have receptors throughout our bodies. These emotion-causing chemicals latch onto organs and tissues throughout our bodies and can affect them in myriad ways.

How are emotions related to the eyes? Research into why we cry is beginning to suggest that crying isn't just an emotional release, but that it also promotes physical health. One series of studies has focused on the biochemical composition of tears. At the Dry Eye and Tear Research Center at the St. Paul-Ramsey Medical Center in Minnesota, researcher William Frey showed subjects a "tearjerker" movie and collected their tears in a small test tube. A few days later, the same subjects returned and were again prompted to cry, this time by being exposed to the aroma of a cut onion. Frey discovered that the emotional tears contained more protein than the tears released as a result of the onion. He also discovered that both kinds contained chemicals released by the body under stress, specifically *adrenocorticotropic hormone (ACTH)* released by the pituitary gland, and *leucine enkephalin,* a morphine-like stress compound that is believed to help mediate pain.

Another stress chemical in tears called *prolactin* may help explain why women cry four times more easily than men. Prolactin is a hormone that helps stimulate the production of milk. Might women cry more often because they have naturally higher levels of this hormone?

This research suggests that one reason we cry might be to decrease the level of stress chemicals that can eventually affect our health. According to this theory, the willingness to cry when under emotional pressure may help prevent stress-related disease. See chapters on specific eye conditions for more information on how emotions affect eye health.

O

Eye disease, like heart disease or arthritis, can also benefit from nontraditional treatments. In the following chapters, we will outline a program of treatment for individual eye diseases that will include all of the holistic modalities we've discussed so far: nutrition, Traditional Chinese Medicine, acupressure, herbs, physical exercise, eye exercises, spinal adjustments and homeopathy. As you will see, expensive drugs and invasive treatments aren't the only way to treat your vision problems.

CHAPTER 2

There's Light at the End of the Tunnel: Treating Glaucoma Holistically

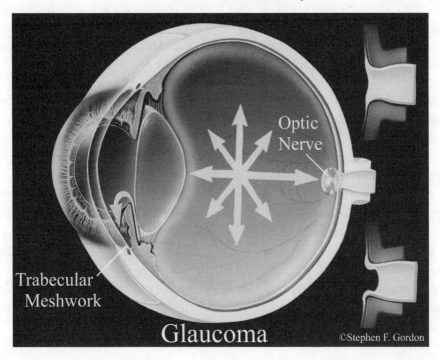

Optic Nerve

Trabecular Meshwork

Glaucoma

©Stephen F. Gordon

Glaucoma (chronic open angle) is an insidious disease that can be difficult to detect until a significant amount of vision is lost. And the reason it is so dangerous is that most glaucoma patients have no symptoms. Many feel no pain at all, and most have 20/20 vision — if only straight ahead. But, left untreated, glaucoma can slowly steal your peripheral vision until you think you're peering through a tunnel (at best) or until you go blind (at worst). Even more frightening is the fact that 70 percent of the vision lost to glaucoma occurs before the patient is diagnosed.

As many as 15 million Americans may have chronic glaucoma. (Only about half of glaucoma patients are ever diagnosed with the disease.[1]) Of those, almost 2 million already suffer some loss of vision, and more than a quarter of a million are blind in at least one eye. Glaucoma costs $2.5 billion each year to treat, and, of course, those numbers will increase as the baby boomer generation ages.

WHAT IS GLAUCOMA?

Technically, glaucoma is due to damage to the optic nerve, sometimes as a result of increased pressure of the *aqueous humor,* the clear, watery fluid that circulates in the chamber of the eye between the cornea and the lens. To understand the disease fully, let's first discuss what happens inside the eye in glaucoma.

Aqueous humor is one of the components of the eyeball that helps transmit light rays to the retina. In the healthy eye, aqueous humor is produced and drained from the eye into the bloodstream at a constant rate so that you always have a fresh supply and always the right amount. The drainage occurs through a little canal between the iris and the cornea.

Sometimes, in some people, too much aqueous humor is produced, and the eye can't get rid of it fast enough to maintain what is called normal *intraocular pressure.* In other patients, the drainage mechanism is faulty; fluid can't escape fast enough to keep pressure down to normal levels. Either way, the abnormally high pressure that results is called *intraocular hypertension.* This increased pressure can damage the optic nerve, first affecting side or peripheral vision, leaving central or straight-ahead vision perfectly normal. If untreated, this central vision is affected as well, and can eventually result in blindness.

Another type of glaucoma is narrow-angle glaucoma. This occurs when there is a sudden increase in the intraocular pressure of the fluid (aqueous humor) inside the eye due to a lack of drainage. The pupil dilates and the iris blocks the normal route of fluid drainage.

Narrow-angle glaucoma is usually more common between the ages of 40 and 60, in people who suffer from hyperopia (farsightedness), and is slightly more common in women.

Narrow-angle glaucoma symptoms are serious and usually include the following:

> Severe pain is felt in or behind the eyes.
> Vision is blurred.
> The whites of the eyes become red.
> Possible nausea or vomiting.

However, just as suddenly and severely as the symptoms appear, they can disappear. Even if the symptoms subside, this form of glaucoma should be treated immediately. Eyedrops will reduce the intraocular pressure, and surgery may need to be performed in order to enlarge the drainage area for the aqueous humor. Treating this type of glaucoma, as well as other rarer forms, such as pigmentary glaucoma, congenital glaucoma and inflammatory glaucoma is not the focus of our holistic approach in this book.

WHO GETS GLAUCOMA?

About 1 in 50 Americans over the age of 40 have chronic open-angle glaucoma, and your risk increases with age. Demographics also play a part: Hispanic-Americans have 20 times the risk of developing glaucoma as white Americans. African-Americans have four times the risk until they reach the age of 45, when their risk increases to almost 17 times more than that of whites.

Health problems, such as obesity and arthritis, can also increase one's risk. Although high blood pressure is not a direct risk factor for glaucoma, many studies have found high blood pressure to be statistically related to glaucoma. This is probably because one factor that can cause high blood pressure is poor circulation. Poor circulation could also prohibit proper eye drainage, possibly causing an increase in ocular pressure, as well as a reduced supply of critical nutrients to the optic nerve. Perhaps this is why glaucoma can result in vision loss at any level of eye pressure if the optic nerve is weak.

HOW DO I KNOW IF I HAVE GLAUCOMA?

The tests for glaucoma are simple and painless. First, your doctor will check for increased intraocular pressure with a *tonometer.* There are two types. The first, called an *applanation tonometer,* measures the pressure with a touch to the cornea. The second type, called an *air puff tonometer,* blows a puff of air at your eyes.

The doctor also will look into your eyes with a *biomicroscope* to evaluate the health of the anterior chamber of the eye. If the chamber is shallow, drainage may not be as efficient as in a normal or deep chamber.

As the doctor looks into your eyes, he or she also will examine the optic nerve for damage, specifically, for a condition called *cupping.* Cupping indicates that the optic nerve has been pushed out of shape by too much pressure from the aqueous humor, or that nerve cells have been lost, leaving empty space behind.

Finally, the doctor will check your peripheral vision with a machine called a visual field tester. This machine detects blind spots in your vision, which determines if there's been any damage from the glaucoma.

Although most physicians believe that intraocular pressure is the only diagnostic indicator of glaucoma, only a complete eye exam that includes evaluation of the pressure, optic nerve, peripheral vision and drainage angle can accurately determine if you are free of glaucoma.

CONVENTIONAL TREATMENTS

In the past few years, there have been new drugs on the market to help lower intraocular pressure. The most common are: Timolol (Timoptic, a beta-blocker), Carteolol (Ocupress), Betaxol (Betoptic), Latanoprost (Xalatan), Brimonidine (Alphagan) and Apraclonidine (Iopidine).

Doctors treating glaucoma try to use the smallest concentration of only one drug and add another drug only if the first isn't working. The beta-blockers are still the most commonly used drugs for glaucoma patients. They work by reducing the amount of aqueous humor that is made by the body.

Timolol (Timoptic) is the most prescribed beta-blocker. Betaxol (Betoptic) is better for patients with pulmonary conditions and also has less likelihood of reducing blood flow (and may even increase blood flow) to the optic nerve than other beta-blockers. It also preserves the visual field equally well or better than other beta-blockers, though its ability to reduce intraocular pressure is somewhat less than other beta-blockers. Side effects are lowered heart rate, anxiety, depression and breathing problems.

Latanoprost (Xalatan) is a prostaglandin analog that lowers intraocular pressure by increasing aqueous humor outflow. It does this by dilating the spaces between the ciliary muscle fibers, thereby increasing the area in which fluid can flow. Its benefits are that you only have to take it once a day and it has fewer side effects than the beta-blockers, the main one being that it darkens the pigment of light-colored irises.

Brimonidine (Alphagan) and Apracoline (Iophidine) lower intraocular pressure by decreasing aqueous humor production and increasing outflow. Their benefits are the same as Latanoprost — you have to take it only once a day. Side effects over time may include allergic reactions, possible dry mouth and fatigue or drowsiness.

GLAUCOMA PREVENTION PROGRAM

Holistic medical treatments can go a long way to help lower your eye pressure and prevent damage from glaucoma. Our comprehensive Glaucoma Prevention Program follows.

The Vision Diet

Studies indicate that glaucoma patients can reduce their eye pressure by five to seven millimeters with an improved diet and supplement program, a reduction as good as or better than that achieved with drugs.[2,3] In general, a diet high in beta-carotene, vitamins C and E and sulfur-bearing amino acids is recommended. Foods containing those nutrients include garlic, onions, beans, spinach, celery, turnips, yellow and orange vegetables, green leafy vegetables, seaweed, apples, oranges and tomatoes.

In addition, drinking lots of water helps maintain the flow of nutrients to the eye and drain metabolic wastes and toxins from eye tissues. Drink 8 to 10 glasses of water a day, but avoid carbonated, caffeinated and alcoholic beverages; they can actually dehydrate eye tissues.

Food Sensitivities, Allergies and Diet

Research into the affects of food allergies on glaucoma patients reveal an important point: It is not simply a matter of inner eye pressure but a complex interaction of biophysical and biochemical parameters that are at work here. A study of 113 patients with chronic simple glaucoma showed immediate intraocular pressure increases of up to 20 millimeters when they were exposed to foods they were allergic to.[4]

One study showed improvement compared to treatment with drugs and surgery or drugs alone. In one case, eye pressure was controlled and vision actually improved once the patient eliminated food allergens from his diet.[5]

There also is evidence that glutamate contributes to glaucoma, so it is best to avoid any foods with monosodium glutamate (MSG).

Vitamins, Minerals and Enzymes

The first step in your nutritional supplement program against glaucoma is to take a broad spectrum multivitamin and mineral supplement. The following are some of the essential nutrients for treating glaucoma. Other recommended nutrients can be found in the Glaucoma Prevention Program at the end of this chapter.

Vitamin A. Vitamin A and carotenoids (also called pro-vitamin A because the body converts them into vitamin A) prevent hydration and swelling of the collagen in the drainage canal of the eye. A deficiency of Vitamin A can affect the outflow of aqueous humor which may result in increased pressure. Glaucoma patients tend to have lower than normal levels of vitamin A.

Vitamin B complex. The entire B complex is important in keeping the eyes healthy.

Vitamin B1. Also called thiamin, vitamin B1 is essential for the health of the optic nerve. Studies have shown that glaucoma patients usually have reduced blood levels of B1 despite normal dietary intake.

Vitamin B3. Vitamin B3 helps keep blood moving by dilating the capillaries and improving the blood flow to and from the eye and the optic nerve.

Vitamin B5. Vitamin B5 strengthens the adrenal glands, important because adrenal hormones help regulate daytime ocular pressure.

Vitamin B6. Also known as *pyridoxine,* vitamin B6 has a diuretic effect which helps decrease eye pressure.

Vitamin B12. Vitamin B12, also called *cobalamin,* seems to improve or prevent the worsening of eyesight in glaucoma patients, apparently by preventing the degeneration of the fatty layer surrounding nerve cells called the *myelin sheath.* Japanese researchers found that a significant number of glaucoma patients who took 1,500 mcg of vitamin B12 for five years actually regained some sight while others showed no deterioration — even though eye pressure did not reduce.[6] No side effects were reported.

Choline. Choline is a member of the vitamin B complex. It acts much like vitamin B3, cleaning out the capillaries and reversing the effects of arteriosclerosis that can contribute to glaucoma.

Inositol. Also part of the B complex, inositol reduces the stress that can contribute to increased intraocular pressure.

Vitamin C. In parts of Europe and Asia, vitamin C is considered routine treatment for glaucoma. Vitamin C lowers eye pressure through a combination of increased blood osmolarity, decreased fluid production and improved outflow of aqueous humor. Plus, it improves collagen metabolism, which may be one of the underlying reasons for the development of glaucoma.

Bioflavonoids (quercetin and rutin). Bioflavonoids are antioxidants found in plant foods that help shore up small blood vessels.

Vitamin E. Another antioxidant, vitamin E helps reduce eye pressure. Choose the natural "d" form, not the synthetic, "dl" form.

Coenzyme Q10. CoQ10, as it's also called, improves heart function and overall blood circulation. With vitamin E, CoQ10 has been proven to benefit glaucoma patients.

Magnesium. Magnesium is a mineral that relaxes smooth muscles and helps prevent muscle spasms. Smooth muscles are what regulate the outflow of aqueous humor from the inner eye.

Spirulina. Spirulina, or blue-green algae, reportedly helps restore vision loss due to glaucoma.

Proteolytic enzymes, such as bromelain, papain and trypsin, help break down proteins that deposit in the eyes' drainage systems, blocking the outflow of aqueous humor and increasing pressure in the eye. These proteins typically accumulate with age, but they also may come from inflammatory processes such as allergy attacks, toxicity and infection. Some food proteins also can exacerbate these deposits, particularly proteins from dairy products, wheat, eggs and soy foods.

Essential fatty acids (EFAs). Refer to chapter 1 for general information on EFAs. In treating glaucoma, EFAs can help reduce the chronic inflammatory processes. Fish and fish oils are rich in omega-3, a polyunsaturated EFA. Studies have shown that Eskimos, who have a high intake of omega-3, have a very low incidence of open angle glaucoma.[7] Studies on animals further confirm that fish oil can reduce fluid pressure within the eyes.[8] The best sources of omega-3 EFAs are the flesh of cold water fish as well as black currant oil, flaxseed and flaxseed oil and hemp seed. We recommend that you either eat fish three times per week or take a supplement.

Omega-6 EFAs are important to protect cells from degenerative changes and to reduce inflammation throughout the body. Sources of omega-6 fatty acids are evening primrose oil, borage oil and black currant oil.

Traditional Chinese Medicine

In Traditional Chinese Medicine, glaucoma is seen primarily as a stagnation or deficiency in the liver meridian, so the herbs and acupressure points prescribed for glaucoma are chosen for their abilities to release the liver qi (energy). They will harmonize the functions of the liver, supporting its ability to promote the smooth flow of energy and blood throughout the body/mind/spirit. In addition, they strengthen the digestion and the functions of the spleen and stomach to help resolve the congealing or stagnation of fluids.

Acupressure

Acupressure is acupuncture without the needles. You won't need to find a practitioner, make an appointment, get time off from work or even go into a medical office. In other words, you can do acupressure yourself. See the Appendix on Acupressure (pages 131–38) for the location and description of the points we recommend for glaucoma.

Daily massage of specific acupressure points can help lower the pressure in the eye by improving drainage of the aqueous humor, lymph, and venous blood. There are seven points that should be manipulated to help improve glaucoma. See Glaucoma Prevention Program, pages 50–51.

Herbal Remedies

Our research has shown that a combination of Chinese, Western and Ayurvedic herbs are helpful in the treatment of chronic glaucoma. The following are the herbs we recommend.

Hsiao Yao Wan (Relaxed Wanderer Pills) is the standard TCM remedy for constrained energy in the liver meridian. These herbs help the liver to spread qi throughout the body and to the eyes. The most important herb in this formula is bupleurum, whose primary role it is to break through obstructions and restore the free flow of energy and blood. The adjunct herbs in this formula — peony root, dong quai, poria fungus, atractylodes, ginger and licorice — support the liver and digestive system. They help relieve dampness, promote digestion and move and disperse stuck energy — exactly what needs to happen for the condition of chronic glaucoma.

Bilberry (Vaccinium myrtillus). Nicknamed "the vision herb," bilberry has accumulated 40 years of research confirming its benefits for the eyes. The constituents responsible for this are called *anthocyanosides*. Bilberry improves the delivery of oxygen and blood to the eye, contains antioxidants for healthy tissues and strengthens the collagen.

Coleus (Coleus forskohlii). Coleus is an herb in the mint family that is traditionally used in Ayurvedic medicine. Studies have shown that coleus will lower intraocular pressure by relaxing smooth muscles in the eye. It also has antihistamine properties, which may reduce the allergic component of increased eye pressure.

Dandelion root (Taraxacum officinalis radix). Another universal liver tonic, dandelion supports the liver, aids in digestion and balances blood sugar levels, which all combine to create good health for the eyes. In addition, dandelion contains antioxidants to help tissue stay healthy.

Eyebright (Euphrasia officinalis). A universal eye tonic, eyebright has been used since the Middle Ages to treat and support vision. It is especially good for eye inflammations, and can be used internally and externally.

Ginger (Zingber officinale). Ginger is an anti-inflammatory that is prescribed for glaucoma patients.

Ginkgo (Ginkgo biloba). Ginkgo has a long, respectable history of use throughout the world for improving the health of the elderly. By increasing blood flow, ginkgo helps provide oxygen and nourishment to the brain, ears, heart and eyes. It's a powerful antioxidant, preventing damage from free radicals, and it appears to stabilize cell membranes, including those of red blood cells, increasing their flexibility and enabling them to squeeze through small capillaries. By supporting and increasing the circulation of the blood to the eyes, this wonderful herb has the potential for more rapid healing of all tissues associated with vision. When taken in combination with blood thinner medication, dosage must be reduced.

Milk Thistle (Silybum marianum). Milk thistle, an excellent liver tonic, increases the flow of bile from the liver, helping to detoxify poisons in our bloodstream. Milk thistle also nourishes the liver, reducing stress and increasing energy throughout the body.

Herbal Tincture for Glaucoma

Combine one to two ounces of the tinctures of bilberry, coleus, dandelion, eyebright, ginkgo, and milk thistle in a large bottle. Take one teaspoon twice a day for three to six months.

   In addition, drink a cup of ginger tea once a day for three to six months.

If taking herbs in capsule form, follow directions by your health care practitioner or follow directions on the label.

A combination formula with all the Chinese, Western and Ayurvedic herbs is available from Integral Health Apothecary and Starfire International (see Resources).

Homeopathic Remedies

Homeopathic remedies must be individualized to the patient's unique set of symptoms; therefore, it is difficult to prescribe the proper remedy without an examination. The following are the homeopathic remedies used most often in the treatment of glaucoma.

Aurum metalicum may be used in treating glaucoma when there is a tendency toward atherosclerosis and suicidal depression.

Gelsemium may be used in treating glaucoma patients who seem apathetic in regard to their visual condition. Their eyelids may appear heavy and droopy.

Phosphorus may be used in treating glaucoma patients who experience a lot of eye fatigue. They may also see green halos around lights and letters may appear red.

Since the underlying causes of glaucoma are often multi-layered and require various remedies at different times, it is especially important in treating glaucoma homeopathically to consult a qualified homeopath (see Resources).

Hormones

Two hormones, epinephrine and melatonin, help regulate intraocular pressure. Conventional medicine uses epinephrine to treat glaucoma because it seems to be the primary daytime eye pressure regulator. Melatonin, secreted by the pineal gland, takes over that job during nighttime.

Adrenal glandulars, including adrenal cortex and other nutritional supports for rebuilding the adrenal function, should be used whenever the adrenals are run down. (They are best taken early in the day.) Vitamin B complex and vitamin C are important adrenal supporters.

Melatonin has become very popular recently, but in the case of glaucoma, it truly is helpful. It reduces the rate of aqueous humor production during sleep and helps glaucoma patients sleep better.[9] (Many people with glaucoma also manifest sleep disturbances.)

Light reduces natural melatonin production, so one way to increase melatonin production naturally is to sleep in total darkness or use a red filter over a night light, which helps the pineal gland sustain melatonin production. This kind of light therapy uses bands of biologically active light, ranging through the spectrum from red to violet. The light is focused into the eyes, where it travels to the brain and activates the autonomic nervous system to regulate disruptions in the system, thereby triggering the healing process. Another way to increase melatonin production is to stimulate the retina with violet light for up to 20 minutes before going to sleep.

We recommend one to three mg of melatonin 30 minutes before bedtime. If you tend to waken during the night, take the time-release version.

Physical Exercise

Exercise is essential for maintaining healthy eyes and vision. Research has shown that glaucoma patients who take a brisk, 40-minute walk five days a week for three months can reduce the pressure in their eyes by approximately 2.5 millimeters — similar to the reduction seen when using beta-blockers.[10] Other studies confirm the importance of whole-body exercise in lowering eye pressure.[11] And the more sedentary you are, the more improvement you will see when you begin to exercise.

An optimal activity program, according to these studies, would include about 45 minutes of nonstop activity — walking, swimming, cycling, rebounding — every other day. Rebounding, as discussed in Chapter 1, is the best exercise to improve blood circulation and lymph drainage. Twelve minutes of rebounding is the aerobic equivalent to 40 minutes of jogging, but with much less strain on the joints and lower back.

Eye Exercises

Certain eye exercises help reduce eye pressure. Frequent eye movements in all directions may help the inner eye drain more efficiently over the long-term, resulting in a decrease in eye pressure. (See eye exercises in Chapter 1, pages 25–29.)

See the Light

Light therapy with the cool colors (blue, blue-green, green, indigo, violet) can stimulate the parasympathetic nervous system into contracting the pupil and increasing drainage of the aqueous humor, resulting in lowered eye pressure. Unfortunately, the fluorescent and incandescent lighting used in most homes and offices are deficient in these colors. Replace lighting at home and at work if possible with full-spectrum lighting.

Deal With Your Emotions

It's not news that your emotions affect your health, and it's also not news that stress exacerbates glaucoma. As early as 1818, researchers linked stress to glaucoma.[12] As a matter of fact, one study found that all of the glaucoma patients involved in the study reported stressful, frustrating life experiences at the time their glaucoma began. During periods when patients' sense of security were most threatened, eye pressure and glaucoma symptoms increased.

That's sobering news for glaucoma patients, but studies also show that chronic stress eventually leads to increased eye pressure even in people without glaucoma.[13] Above-average stress has been shown to increase the risk for high eye pressure by almost three times.[14] It appears that eye pressure is never elevated in happy, tranquil people.

Stress causes dilation of the pupil, which increases inner eye pressure. It also raises blood pressure, which, as we've already discussed, is associated with glaucoma.

Reducing stress is important for everyone, of course, but particularly so for the glaucoma patient, because the glaucoma-prone individual tends to have a personality that's just ripe for a stressful life: Studies show that glaucoma patients tend to be perfectionists, nervous, anxiety-ridden and/or hypersensitive.[15] If you already have those personality traits working against you, take some of these steps to relieve the pressure on you and on your eyes.

Reducing the stress in your life and living more harmoniously will reduce the internal pressure that produces anger and frustration, the emotions most associated with glaucoma. Instead of suppressing anger, feel it, but don't fear it. Don't indulge in it, but learn when to express it and when to say nothing. Work on increasing your sense of self, so that you will be less vulnerable to impatience and touchiness. Slowing down and acting from an inner stillness and strength can slowly reduce anger and impatience.

Try meditation, tai chi, yoga or psychotherapy. Learn biofeedback techniques. This can be as simple as making sure you relax and smile a few times a day.

Other Treatments

Probably the glaucoma treatment that people are most curious about is marijuana. Smoking marijuana does reduce eye pressure. Used topically, just a drop of *tetrahydrocannabinol,* the active ingredient in marijuana, applied to the eye helps the pressure drop for about five hours, which is similar to conventional anti-glaucoma eye drops.[16]

Smoking tobacco, on the other hand, can raise the pressure in the eyes and dramatically reduce blood circulation.

Even your clothing can affect eye pressure. For example, neckties can increase eye pressure by compressing the jugular veins, reducing blood drainage from the head and eyes. In one study, 67 percent of the businessmen examined wore their neckties tight enough to reduce visual performance.[17] Loosen your necktie, particularly if you have glaucoma or are at risk for the disease; you really don't need that added stress.

CASE STUDIES

Dr. Swartwout

While a student doctor of optometry, the co-author of this book discovered that he had elevated intraocular pressure (26 in each eye) and some loss of peripheral vision surrounding a blind spot — an early sign of glaucoma. Because he preferred a natural, preventive approach to a lifetime of suppressive eyedrops with side effects, he tried a combination of natural therapies. These included removal of amalgam fillings (a source of toxic metal), nutritional and homeopathic remedies, and Syntonic treatment (stimulation of the retina with selected frequencies of visible light) with indigo light therapy. After one year of these therapies, his eye pressure went down to normal (15 in each eye), with no further loss of vision.

In another case, a retired physician with glaucoma decided to forgo the eyedrops prescribed by his doctor when he was told they weren't expected to work. (They were prescribed, however, because they were covered by his insurance plan.) Instead, the man took the herb coleus (*Coleus forskohlii*), often prescribed in India to bring down eye pressure, which is exactly what it did—from 42 and 46 to 30 and 31 — within four days.

Trish P.

Trish, a 58-year-old Caucasian woman, came in for her annual comprehensive eye exam. Her only symptom was that her current reading glasses felt a little weak. Her distance visual acuity without glasses was 20/20 right eye, 20/20 left eye and 20/20 with both eyes. Her near visual acuity with her current glasses was 20/25 right eye, 20/25 left eye and 20/25 with both eyes at a distance of 16 inches.

Her eyes were not corrected for distance and at near her prescription was

+2.50 in both eyes, which gave her 20/20 in both eyes at near. Her previous prescription was +2.00 in both eyes. Her optic nerve was normal and the rest of her retinal evaluation looked healthy.

A test called tonometry, which tests the intraocular pressure of the eyes, was done and showed a pressure of 26 mm HG in the right eye and 27 in the left eye. These pressures are slightly above normal (12–24 mm Hg). Due to the fact that the intraocular pressure was above normal, a visual field test was done to evaluate her peripheral vision. This test also proved to be within normal findings. There were no signs of any other medical problems — no diabetes, no high blood pressure, no obesity.

The conventional treatment for this case would be a slight increase in the reading glasses prescription to +2.50 for each eye. Except for the intraocular pressure, everything else was normal. Since high pressure could be an indication of early glaucoma, further testing would be done.

There were three possible choices:

1. Trish could come back for more eye pressure tests and visual field tests, and if these were within normal limits she would be told to come back in one year.

2. If the eye pressures continued to be slightly above normal (which labels her as a glaucoma suspect), Trish would be re-evaluated on a three-month basis as long as all other tests were normal.

3. If the eye pressures and/or other tests were not within normal limits, it would indicate glaucoma. She would need treatment, and, if seeing a conventional opthalmologist, it would probably be in the form of beta-blocker eye drops such as Timoptic, the mildest way to hopefully control, but not cure, the glaucoma.

If the pressure did not go down while on the drops, a checkup every three months would make sure that any increase would be found before it did any damage. If the pressure did increase, the doctor would prescribe stronger eye drops; and if that didn't work, other pills to control intraocular pressure would be prescribed.

In most cases, open-angle glaucoma can be safely and effectively treated with medication. In rare cases when this is not possible, surgery can be done.

In co-author Dr. Marc Grossman's office, the treatment strategy used with Trish included choices 1 and 2 above in conjunction with some of the recommendations in the Glaucoma Prevention Program. During the past six years Trish's eye pressure has stabilized to approximately 17 (right eye) and 16 (left eye), and she has never had to be on any medication for her eyes.

GLAUCOMA PREVENTION PROGRAM

Vision Diet

Follow the Vision Diet in Chapter 1 as closely as possible.

- Beneficial foods include fresh fruits and vegetables (especially kale, collards, mustard greens and spinach) and cold water fish such as salmon, mackerel or sardines.
- Avoid refined sugars, artificial sweeteners, fried foods, excess fats (especially saturated and hydrogenated fats), alcohol, caffeinated and carbonated beverages.
- Drink 8–10 glasses of water per day, but not with food — 30 minutes before a meal or 2 hours after a meal.

Nutritional Supplements

Take the following vitamins and minerals on a daily basis:

Vitamin A	10,000 I.U.	Rutin	300 mg
Beta-carotene	25,000 I.U.	Magnesium	500 mg
Vitamin B1 (thiamin)	100 mg	Calcium	500 mg for men, 800 mg for women
B2 (riboflavin)	100 mg	Coenzyme Q10	100 mg
B3 (niacin)	100 mg	L-Carnitine	500 mg
B5 (pantothenic acid)	500 mg	Garlic	1,000 mg
		Coleus (*forskolin*)	200 mg
B6 (pyroxidine)	100 mg	Bilberry	300 mg
Folic acid	1,000 mcg	Omega-3 Oils	1,500 mg
B12 (cobalamin)	100 mcg	Omega-6 Oils	1,500 mg
Choline	100 mg	Ginkgo Biloba	240 mg
Inositol	100 mg	Zinc	30 mg
Biotin	500 mcg	Selenium	200 mcg
Vitamin C	3,000 mg	N-acetyl-cysteine	1,000 mg
Vitamin D	200 I.U.	Alpha lipoic acid	200 mg
Vitamin E	800 I.U.	Spirulina	20,000 USP units
Quercetin	2,000 mg	proteolytic enzymes	3 times a day

Acupressure Points

Massage each point for 30 seconds, twice a day:

1. Bladder 1 (*Jing Ming*)
2. Gall bladder 20 (*Feng Chi*)

3. Large intestine 4 (*Hegu*)
4. Liver 3 (*Taichang*)
5. Stomach 1 (*Cheng qi*)
6. *Qiuhou*
7. Bladder 18 (*Gan Shu*)
See the Appendix, pp. 131–38 for location of points.

Herbal Remedies

Take the combination formula of Chinese, Western and Ayurvedic herbs (Hsiao Wan Yao plus other herbs) available from Integral Health Apothecary and Starfire International (see Resources). Take 12 Hsiao Wan Yao pills and 1 teaspoon of the combination herb tincture twice per day.

Homeopathic Remedies

Consult a trained homeopath who can recommend the appropriate constitutional remedy for you to alleviate your glaucoma.

Exercises

Do 20 minutes of both aerobic and eye exercises at least four times per week (see Chapter 1).

Spinal Manipulation

Consult a qualified chiropractor or osteopath to make sure that the spine and neck are free from any energy blocks that might cause poor circulation and, thus, lack of energy to the eyes.

Light

Wear blue-green and/or indigo color therapy glasses 20 minutes per day. Also, if possible, contact a doctor trained in Syntonic Therapy (light/color therapy for vision conditions). See Resources.

Emotional Health

The emotions most associated with glaucoma are stress, suppressed anger and frustration. Try meditation, tai chi, yoga, psychotherapy or biofeedback techniques to reduce stress.

CHAPTER 3

Through a Lens Clearly: Preventing and Treating Cataracts

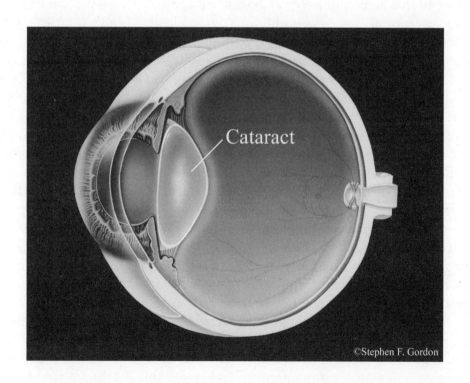

Cataract

©Stephen F. Gordon

Cataracts can probably best be described as an opaque spot on the lens of the eye that you cannot see through. At best, you seem to be looking through a cloud or a haze, and this haze can vary in size, density and location. Therefore, its effect on your vision will also vary. Many people experience a general reduction in vision at first; they need more light to read by, or they have difficulty with street signs when they're driving. A cataract also can affect depth perception. This can be a particular danger to older people who risk greater injury from falls and accidents.

Cataracts tend to worsen over time. They are the major cause of blindness in the world. Almost 40 million people — about 4 million in the United States — suffer from cataracts. Indeed, it is the most common surgical procedure covered by Medicare with almost 600,000 surgeries per year. And most of those surgeries are for older patients. Only 15 percent of people are affected with cataracts by age 55, but this figure jumps to 50 percent by age 75, and 90 percent by age 85.

However, of all the eye conditions covered in this book, cataracts are the most amenable to treatment by conventional medical methods. The standard treatment is to remove the lens by a technique called *phacoemulsification*. A surgeon uses an ultrasonic beam to break up the hard lens, and then vacuums up the pieces from the eye with a suction device. An artificial lens, called an *intraocular lens* or *IOL,* is inserted to replace the cataract lens.

We recommend surgery to our cataract patients who have severe vision loss. At the same time, it is important to understand that a cataract is a symptom of an underlying condition; it is a sign that the natural processes of your body are breaking down on some level, and that the normal flow of nutrients into the eye and waste products out of the eye has been compromised. It is vitally important to treat the underlying condition that causes the cataract. Even people preparing for cataract surgery should seek to improve their overall health before they go through this invasive procedure. Because cataracts progress slowly over many years, there is usually time for preventive measures to be quite successful.

In the early stages, it may not be necessary to have surgery. Nutritional and other complementary medical treatments can slow and even reverse the growth of cataracts. In this chapter, we will review the natural methods that we have found to be most effective in treating cataracts. We also will present a case history of a patient whose vision improved and then stabilized through a regimen of natural care. And we will put the contributing factors of this common eye condition in perspective.

WHAT CAUSES CATARACTS?

Free radicals are responsible for most cataracts. Free radicals are natural byproducts of metabolism. These highly reactive chemicals cause oxidation, which in turn causes aging. As the lens of the eye ages, it hardens and loses its ability to focus. This process is similar to hardening of the arteries, and it is often associated with similar changes in the joints. But other things — such as dental problems, physical injury to the vertebrae or neck or any stress which reduces eye movement and increases muscle tension — can also cause cataracts. Food allergies or sensitivities, particularly involving dairy products, wheat and soy, can congest the sinuses, impairing lymphatic and veinous drainage, resulting in decreased nutrition to the eyes with cataracts the result. Toxins, pharmaceutical drugs, smoking and diabetes also are major causes.

CATARACT PREVENTION PROGRAM

Our cataract prevention program emphasizes our basic regimen for good eye health with a few special suggestions.

The Effects of Toxins

Many synthetic chemicals and pharmaceuticals can cause cataracts. Steroids, for example, both those taken internally and those applied to the skin, are a typical cause of cataracts, because they block the normal metabolism of connective tissue of which the lens is comprised.

Other toxic compounds implicated in the formation of cataracts are naphthalene (mothballs), acetone, nitrogen mustard, and paradichlorobenzol, an insecticide. Drugs that can cause cataracts include tranquilizers, corticosteroids (such as Prednisone and cortisone), oral contraceptives, and pilocarpine and phospholine iodine, two drugs taken by glaucoma patients.

Cigarette smoking causes about 20 percent of all cataracts. Men who smoke more than a pack a day increase their risk for cataracts by 205 percent; for female smokers, risk increases 63 percent.[1,2] Surprisingly, quitting without supplementing your diet with additional vitamins and minerals doesn't seem to eliminate risk for almost ten years, probably due to the fact that smoking depletes antioxidant levels in the eye.

Toxins in our environment and in our food also are implicated in the formation of cataracts. Heavy metals, particularly mercury, are found in high levels in people with cataracts. Mercury is retained in the lens longer than in any other tissue in the body since it binds to the sulfur in protein and the lens has the densest protein in the body. Mercury, which accumulates in tuna, swordfish, shark, striped bass and pike, is now considered a common trigger for cataracts.[3] Other heavy metals implicated in cataract risk are cadmium, bromine, cobalt, iridium, nickel, iron and lead. Chelation therapy can be helpful in reducing the burden of heavy metals in the body.

The Vision Diet

The Vision Diet outlined in Chapter 1, along with lots of water and supplementation, helps maintain a healthy lens that easily drains away metabolic wastes and toxins from eye tissues. Whenever possible, a nutritional program should be maintained for at least three or four months before considering cataract surgery.[4] In addition, it is clearly beneficial to maintain a low-calorie diet. Animal studies show that cutting calories 20 to 40 percent results in a 30 to 50 percent reduction in cataracts, as well as a 30 percent increase in longevity, increased immune function and decreased risk of cancer. Let's examine some nutrition guidelines for a healthy lens.

Cut back on sugar or, better yet, eliminate it completely from your diet. High levels of sugar in the blood contribute to cataract formation, so it's not surprising that diabetics are at three to four times the risk for cataracts. Blood sugar interferes with the lens' ability to pump out excess fluid from the eye and maintain its clarity; with too much sugar, this is difficult and sometimes impossible. Cataract prevention is especially important for diabetics, because diabetic retinopathy can accelerate for six months following cataract surgery.

All types of sugars, not just white sugar, can impair the lens' ability to keep itself clear. Even milk sugar, or lactose, found in all dairy products, can contribute to cataracts, destroying glutathione and vitamin C levels in the lens.

Drink lots of water — eight to ten glasses a day — to maintain the flow of nutrients to the lens and the release of wastes and toxins from tissues.

Eat foods high in beta-carotene, vitamins C and E and sulfur-bearing amino acids. These substances are called *antioxidants,* and most of the nutritional components of cataract prevention and reversal are related to boosting antioxidant defenses. Antioxidants are one of the most important ways to combat *free radicals,* which are a major cause of cataract formation. A good diet, supplemented with antioxidant vitamins and minerals, can help prevent oxidation.

Foods high in antioxidants include garlic, onions, beans, yellow and orange vegetables, spinach and other green, leafy vegetables, celery, seaweed, apples, carrots, tomatoes, turnips and oranges.

Some foods, particularly dairy products, wheat and soy foods, can exacerbate eye problems by causing sinus congestion which can impair lymph and blood drainage from the area around the eyes. When lymph and blood can't flow in and out of the eyes, nutrients don't reach the eyes, and toxins and metabolic wastes aren't eliminated. Try avoiding these foods for a month to see whether you are less congested. Then re-introduce them one at a time to help you identify your specific problem foods.

Vitamins and Minerals

Taking a good optimum potency multivitamin is an important foundation of any cataract prevention program. The following are some of the essential nutrients for treating cataracts. Other recommended nutrients can be found in the Cataract Prevention Program at the end of this chapter.

Vitamin C. The king of the antioxidants and the vitamin we emphasize most in our practice for cataract patients, it has long been known that vitamin C can both prevent and heal cataracts. In addition to its other benefits, vitamin C can reverse the negative effects of sugar on cataract formation, according to studies undertaken since 1935.

The normal, healthy lens contains a higher level of vitamin C than any other organ except the adrenal glands. However, when cataracts are forming, the vitamin C level is very low and sometimes nonexistent. Similarly, the vitamin C level in the aqueous humor which supplies nutrition to the lens is also low when cataracts are forming. This overall reduction of vitamin C is due both to the eye's impaired ability to secrete vitamin C into the aqueous humor as well as to the body's overall vitamin C deficiency when cataracts are forming. Vitamin C has another surprising effect on the eyes: in studies since 1935, vitamin C has been shown to prevent and even reverse the negative effects of sugar on the eyes.[5]

Injection of vitamin C into the blood or aqueous humor resulted in improved vision in 70 percent of the study subjects.[3] And study subjects who took vitamin C daily for at least five years reduced their risk for cataracts by 70 percent.[6] Some patients in the studies showed measurable improvement within two weeks.

Vitamin A and beta-carotene. Vitamin A and its precursor, beta-carotene, are particularly important for eye health. People with low levels of beta-carotene stand seven times the risk of contracting cataracts as those with high levels. Beta-carotene, like vitamin C, also may act as a light filter for the eyes, protecting against photooxidation of the lens.

Although vitamin A can be toxic in excess, there is no risk of toxicity from beta-carotene.

Bioflavonoids. Bioflavonoids, such as quercetin and rutin, are important antioxidants that are synergistic with vitamin C. They need each other's presence to work efficiently. Quercetin seems to be the most effective in the prevention of cataracts.

Vitamin B complex. The B vitamins work together synergistically, and excesses of one B vitamin can cause a deficiency of another, so we recommend that you take a B vitamin complex that contains a minimum daily dose of 100 to 150 mg of each B vitamin.

Calcium. Animal studies have shown that a diet deficient in calcium can bring on cataracts.[7]

Chromium. Chromium helps regulate blood sugar and improves blood circulation. Patients with cataracts have been found to have only about 40 percent of the chromium they need.

Copper and zinc. People with cataracts are almost always deficient in copper and zinc, two minerals that work hand-in-hand in cataract prevention and treatment. Copper stimulates the production of *superoxide dismutase,* an antioxidant enzyme, but only when the body has enough zinc for the reaction. Zinc deficiency can actually cause cataracts in humans and animals. And zinc makes sure the body can assimilate vitamin A. It's also important for the health of the epithelium of the lens and for the metabolism of sugar within the lens tissue.

Vitamin E. Like low levels of beta-carotene, a low level of vitamin E also increases cataract risk and reduces photooxidation.[8,9] A daily dose of 800 I.U. has been shown to reduce cataract risk by up to 56 percent.

Manganese. Along with copper and zinc, manganese is also involved in the production of superoxide dismutase.

Magnesium. Magnesium helps regulate sugar levels and proper nerve function, as well as vitamin B6 metabolism.

Potassium. Potassium is important for circulation, fluid balance and detoxification.

Selenium. Selenium gives vitamin E a jumpstart and also helps protect the lens from mercury damage.

ADDITIONAL SUPPLEMENTS

Proteolytic enzymes (papain or bromelain). The lens of the eye is the most concentrated protein in the body, and insufficient intake or digestion of too much protein can cause cataracts. Most Americans, with the exception of vegetarians, eat two to three times more protein than they need. We suggest taking the enzyme bromelain or papain to assist in protein digestion. Papain works better for most people.

Sulfur. In its organic forms, sulfur is one of the most important elements for good vision. It is a critical part of glutathione, a powerful antioxidant on the front line of the detoxification process in the liver, particularly in the elimination of mercury, a common trigger of cataracts. Glutathione has been linked to lens health since the early 1900s; in one study, injections of glutathione improved lens clarity in 30 percent of the patients. Sulfur also is a component of many enzymes, including the enzyme that pumps excess fluid out of the lens to maintain its clarity.

Several forms of organic sulfur are beneficial for vision. One is methyl sulfonyl methane (MSM), a crystalline powder that can be added to water or other drinks. Take ½ teaspoon per 100 pounds of body weight twice a day. Another form of organic sulfur is N-acetyl-cysteine (NAC), which can dramatically boost the body's level of L-glutathione.

Taurine. Taurine has also been shown to be helpful in cataract prevention.

Traditional Chinese Medicine

In Traditional Chinese Medicine, senile cataracts are often seen as a result of a deficiency in the kidney and liver meridians. This causes a lack of energy and blood flowing to the eyes, which leads to poor nutrition of the eyes, thus causing an opaqueness of the lens. The spleen meridian also plays a role in the nourishment of the eyes, and if dysfunctional, it can also cause cataracts.

The herbs and acupressure points prescribed for cataracts are chosen for their ability to tone both the kidney and liver qi. By strengthening the energies of the kidney, liver and spleen, an overall improvement in the body's immune system and energy is promoted, thus allowing more available healing energy to come to the eyes.

Acupressure

Each of the 365 acupuncture points in the body has a unique energy or essence. See the Cataract Prevention Program, page 67 for the relevant points for preventing and healing cataracts.

Herbal Remedies

To an herbalist, you are more than an interesting set of symptoms that must be eradicated with the proper medicine; rather, you are a complex human being functioning on a mental, emotional, spiritual and physical level. Since cataracts are indicative of deficiencies in the kidney and liver meridians, we have found that a combination of Chinese and Western herbs is effective for the treatment of cataracts.

Lycii-Rehmannia formula. The Chinese formula Lycii-Rehmannia contains rehmannia root, cornus fruit, dioscorea root, alisma root, poria fungus, moutan, lycium berry and chrysanthemum flowers. This formula works to nurture the vital essence of the kidneys by relieving dampness and helping the yin energies (water, fluids) to support the body, mind and spirit and heal the eyes. This combination is a classic tonic for visual problems associated with a yin-deficient condition — one in which there is excessive heat and/or dryness, such as dry, irritated and/or itchy eyes or photophobia (light sensitivity).

American ginseng (Panax quinquefolium) is a tonic particularly good for the adrenal glands. American ginseng is gentler than the Asian varieties; it has more of a yin function. American ginseng supports the immune system, provides energy and balances blood sugar levels.

Bilberry (Vaccinium myrtillus) appears to play a significant role in the prevention of cataracts. In one study, a combination of bilberry and vitamin E stopped cataract formation in 97 percent of the patients — without side effects.[10] Bilberry also may strengthen the collagen that supports eye structure. An antioxidant, it protects the lens from oxidation.

Ginkgo (Ginkgo biloba) has been called the elixir of youth for its powerful effects on improving memory and brain function, protecting the heart and restoring blood circulation, improving hearing and vision and maintaining good health and general vitality. It's a powerful antioxidant as well and has been shown to increase blood circulation to the brain.

Shou Wu nourishes the power that makes birth, development and maturation graceful. It is a tonifying herb used in this context for fading vision.

Cataract Formula

Mix one to two ounces of each of these herb tinctures together and take one teaspoon twice a day.

A combination formula of these Chinese and Western herbs is available from Integral Health Apothecary and Starfire International (see Resources).

Homeopathic Remedies

Homeopathic remedies must be individualized to each patient's unique set of symptoms; therefore, it can be difficult to prescribe the proper remedy without an examination. The following are the homeopathic remedies used most often in the treatment of cataracts.

Calcarea carbonicum is especially good for those who are sensitive to dampness and cold, and who are fair-skinned and overweight. Their diet might produce an excessively acidic chemical imbalance.

Causticum is often used for those who have a heaviness in their upper eyelids. They may also have warts on their upper lid and may experience burning, itching and a sandy feeling in the eyes even though no conjunctivitis is present. Sensitivity to cold air blowing on the eyes and to cold drinks is also symptomatic.

Cineraria maritima (the homeopathic version of *succus cineraria maritima,* see below) is used for beginning cataracts.

Pulsatilla is indicated for those who are fair-skinned, easily brought to tears and with a tendency toward depression.

When treating cataracts homeopathically, we recommend that you consult a qualified homeopath.

Medications

There is a pharmaceutical drug that is helpful for early stage cataracts. Succus cineraria maritima, a medication listed in the *Physicians Desk Reference for Ophthalmology*, is a solution of the total extracts of fresh cineraria with *homamilis vulgaris* (witch hazel) and boric acid. Applying drops of succus cineraria to the eye increases the circulation in the intraocular tissues, also stimulating collateral circulation and the normal metabolism of the eye.

Clinical observation has shown that succus cineraria is helpful in limiting the progression of existing cataract formation. The earlier one begins treatment, the more effective it is. We recommend using this medication even past the beginning stages if a cataract operation is not possible. Succus cineraria maritima is available from your physician or as a homeopathic from your homeopath.

Physical Exercise

Reducing body mass index reduces cataract risk, and exercise helps improve body mass index. In addition to the other exercises mentioned in Chapter 1, a good yet gentle form of exercise is rebounding, bouncing on a mini-trampoline. Rebounding stimulates lymphatic drainage of the entire body without stressing the joints or the cardiovascular system. See page 25 for a discussion of rebounding.

Eye Exercises

Certain eye exercises can also help to bring energy and blood to the eyes, thus helping to drain away toxins or congestion from the eyes. See the eye exercises in Chapter 1.

Avoid Microwaves

Radiation leakage from microwave ovens are a direct cause of cataracts, so avoid constant peeking into the oven door window while you cook. In addition, food proteins exposed to microwaves can become toxic to the lens which is made mostly of protein.

Similarly, ultraviolet light from the sun can cause cumulative damage to the lens, so always wear a hat and a good pair of sunglasses when you're out in the sun.

Emotional Health

Managing your emotional health is very important in maintaining physical health. Fear (fear of failure, fear of responsibility, fear of being alone, fear of death, etc.) is at the root of many of life's problems, and is a major factor in the development of cataracts. In order to deal with fear, you need to slowly and gradually build self-confidence by completing tasks of increasing difficulty and challenge. But, be careful not to go beyond your abilities, or discouragement and depression may ensue.

To manage fear effectively, it is important to find a source of inner strength and peace, and then learn to act from this inner stillness and strength, rather than from restlessness and fear. Learning the balance between activity and rest and learning how to be, as well as how to do, are crucial parts of managing fear.

Recommended activities for fear management include meditation, yoga, qi gong, tai chi and psychotherapy.

CASE STUDY

Esther

Esther was in the early stages of cataract formation. A retail shopkeeper for 35 years, Esther didn't get a lot of exercise; most of her working hours were spent sitting or standing behind the counter. She smoked and drank several cups of coffee a day. Esther liked sweets and her daily diet included pastry, desserts, soda and seltzer, plus red meat, chicken and turkey. She ate vegetables only three or four times a week and fruit only occasionally. At 5 feet, 1 inch tall, she weighed 135 pounds.

Our regimen for Esther included:

1. Stop smoking.

2. Exercise at least 20 minutes a day, four days a week.

3. Eye exercises.

4. A radical change in diet. Eliminate coffee, sugar and soda; eat more vegetables and fruit and less red meat. Drink at least eight glasses of water a day.

5. A vitamin and mineral formula that included: beta-carotene, vitamin C, quercetin, vitamin E, B complex, folic acid, B6, riboflavin, B1, selenium, zinc, copper, manganese, magnesium, calcium, potassium, iron, chromium, glutathione and N-acetyl-cysteine.

6. A Chinese herbal formula that included Lycii-Rehmannia with bilberry, American ginseng and ginkgo biloba.

7. Acupressure for five to ten minutes a day.

8. Wearing a hat and UV-blocking sunglasses outdoors.

We designed this program to slow the progression of Esther's cataracts and hopefully reduce them, thereby improving her vision. The program also would improve her cardiovascular and circulatory systems, which in turn would decrease her susceptibility to heart disease and cancer and, in general, make her a healthier person.

It was a great success. Soon after beginning the program, Esther's eyesight improved to what it had been before the cataracts. Ten years later, Esther is healthy, and her vision has stabilized. She has never needed cataract surgery.

CATARACT PREVENTION PROGRAM

Vision Diet

Follow the Vision Diet in Chapter 1 as closely as possible.

- Beneficial foods include fresh fruits (especially apples and pineapples), vegetables (especially carrots and spinach) and cold water fish such as salmon, mackerel and sardines.
- Avoid refined sugars, dairy, fried foods, margarine and excess protein from red meat.
- Drink 8–10 glasses of water per day, but not with food — 30 minutes before a meal or 2 hours after a meal.

Nutritional Supplements

Take the following vitamins and minerals on a daily basis:

Vitamin A	5,000–10,000 I.U.
Beta-carotene	25,000 I.U.
Vitamin B1 (thiamin)	100 mg
B2 (riboflavin)	100 mg
B3 (niacin)	100 mg
B5 (pantothenic acid)	500 mg
B6 (pyroxidine)	100 mg
Folic acid	1,000 mcg
B12 (cobalamin)	100 mcg
Choline	100 mg
Inositol	100 mg
Biotin	500 mcg
Vitamin C	3,000 mg. (buffered form)
Vitamin D	200 I.U.
Vitamin E	800 I.U.
Zinc	30 mg
Chromium	200 mcg
Bilberry	300 mg
Selenium	200 mcg

Calcium	500 mg for men, 800 mg for women
Magnesium	500 mg
Alpha lipoic acid	200 mg
N-acetyl-cysteine (NAC)	1,000 mg
Quercetin	2,000 mg
Rutin	300 mg
Ginkgo biloba (24% extract)	160 mg*
Coenzyme Q10	100 mg
L-Glutathione	50 mg
Taurine	500 mg
Manganese	20 mg
Copper	2 mg
Potassium	100 mg
Vanadium	200 mcg

*Take 40 mg if you are taking any blood thinner medication.

Acupressure Points

Massage each point for 30 seconds, twice a day:

1. Bladder 1 (*Jing Ming*)
2. Bladder 2 (*Zan Zhu*)
3. Gall Bladder 1 (*Tong Zi Liao*)
4. Gall Bladder 37 (*Guang Ming*)
5. Large Intestine 4 (*He Gu*)
6. *Qiuhou*
7. Stomach 36 (*Zu San Li*)
8. *Yu Yao*
9. Kidney 3 (*Taixi*)
10. Spleen 6 (*Sanyinjiao*)
11. Bladder 23 (*Shen Shu*)

See Appendix for location of points

Herbal Remedies

Take the combination formula of Chinese and Western herbs (Lycii-Rehmannia plus other herbs) available from Integral Health Apothecary and Starfire International (see Resources). Or take 8 Lycii-Rehmannia pills 3 times a day, 12 twice a day, or 1 dropper full of tincture twice a day plus the Cataract Formula on page 62.

Homeopathic Remedies	Consult a trained homeopath who can recommend the appropriate constitutional remedy for you with regard to your cataracts.
Medications	Apply Succus cineraria maritima directly into the cataract eye, 2 drops morning and evening, or as directed by your physician or homeopath.
Exercises	Do 20 minutes of both aerobic and eye exercises at least four times per week (see Chapter 1).
Spinal Manipulation	Consult a qualified chiropractor or osteopath to make sure that the spine and neck are free from any energy blocks that might cause poor circulation and, thus, lack of energy to the eyes.
Emotional Health	The emotion most associated with cataracts is fear. Try meditation, tai chi, yoga, qi gong, tai chi, biofeedback techniques or psychotherapy.

CHAPTER 4

Lifting the Fog:
Macular Degeneration

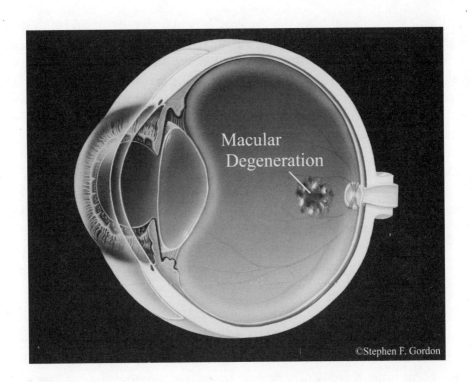

Macular
Degeneration

©Stephen F. Gordon

As recently as a year or two ago, it would have been hard to find an article on macular degeneration in the mainstream media. But, since we began writing this book, there have been half a dozen reports on this disease, and we expect to see more as the Baby Boomers continue to age. Today, macular degeneration is the leading cause of irreversible blindness. By the year 2020, an estimated 7.5 million Americans will suffer significant vision loss due to macular degeneration. In all, over 15 million Americans have signs of macular degeneration, with 167,000 new cases added each year. Although there is no effective treatment yet, natural remedies can go a long way in preventing the disease from progressing to the point of vision loss.

WHAT IS MACULAR DEGENERATION?

How do you know if you have the disease? Macular degeneration is the slow deterioration of the cells in the *macula,* a tiny, yellowish area near the center of the retina where vision is the most acute. This deterioration therefore affects your central vision, the very vision you use for reading, writing, driving and identifying faces. When you have macular degeneration, straight lines become crooked, distinct shapes are blurry, lines become wavy, and there is fog in the center of your vision. However, your peripheral vision is not affected.

There are two types of macular degeneration: Ninety percent of people with macular degeneration have the *dry* type, in which small, yellow spots called *drusen* form underneath the macula. The drusen slowly break down the cells in the macula, causing distorted vision. Dry macular degeneration can progress to the second, more severe type, called *wet* macular degeneration.

In the wet type, new, abnormal blood vessels begin to grow toward the macula. These new blood vessels may leak blood and fluid that further deteriorate the macula, causing rapid and severe vision loss.

CONVENTIONAL TREATMENT

At the present time, there is no effective treatment. Some causes of wet macular degeneration are treated with laser surgery, but the treatment itself may not effectively seal up a leaky blood vessel without at the same time permanently destroying retinal nerve fibers that pass through the area. According to the National Eye Institute, laser treatment can actually worsen vision, and any ability to slow the progression of disease does not appear until at least a year after surgery.[1]

As always, prevention is the best medicine. Since less than one percent of those with macular degeneration have progressed to the point of legal blindness, most are in a position to benefit greatly from prevention.

RISK FACTORS

Who is at risk for macular degeneration? Everyone experiences the disease somewhat. Long before one becomes aware of the disease, the macula begins to deteriorate. In normal individuals, the macula begins to deteriorate from youth through age 30; deterioration accelerates after the age of 50. By age 65, the incidence of macular degeneration increases.

People with drusen on the retina also are at risk. Drusen begin to appear on the retina between the ages of 30 and 60; after that, the spots form more rapidly, increasing the risk of macular degeneration.

People with macular degeneration in one eye are at high risk for degeneration in the other eye. Within four years of developing it in one eye, 23 percent will develop it in the other eye. Plus, people with the dry form of the disease are at risk for developing the wet form if their retinal arteries become occluded. Any patient with macular degeneration should have an Amsler Grid home test. (See page 72.) This will help them notice the first sign of progressive vision loss.

If you have cataracts, you are at risk for macular degeneration. Dense cataracts are associated with a 50 percent increase in the risk of macular degeneration; slight cataracts increase the risk by 80 percent. But cataract surgery increases your chances of macular degeneration 200 percent because your eyes have less protection from sunlight, which is also a risk factor. In a five-year period, the retinas of patients who had cataracts removed showed accelerated aging equivalent to 30 years of normal aging.[2]

High-risk patients are blue-eyed, have drusen on their retina (about 30 percent of adults) and a family history of macular degeneration. These people should take preventive measures; they should quit smoking, give up coffee, stay out of excessive exposure to sunlight and eat a nutrient-rich diet.

Smoking must be completely avoided. Compared to nonsmokers, smokers have 2½ times the risk of developing macular degeneration.[3] The average age at which smokers are affected is 64 versus 71 for nonsmokers, so quitting smoking could add seven years of good vision to your life. What exactly does smoking do? It stresses nerve cells like those in the macula, because nicotine destabilizes nerve

Amsler Grid

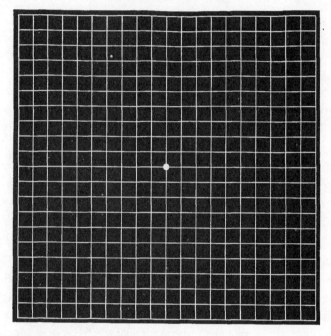

Directions for Amsler Grid

Hold the grid at your normal reading distance. Use glasses if needed. Cover your left eye and look at the dot in the center. Observe if all the lines look straight and even, or if any are wavy and distorted. Are any pieces of the grid missing? Now, cover your right eye and repeat the above directions. Recheck as often as your eye care practitioner recommends. If there are any abnormalities, contact your eye care practitioner immediately.

cell membranes. Smoking also reduces the quality of blood circulation both by triggering vasoconstriction and by increasing cholesterol levels. In addition, smoking deprives the body of vitamin C, a potent antioxidant, which has been shown to protect the eyes from retinal damage caused by sunlight.

Caffeine also is no friend to your eyes because it impairs nerve cell health and the quality of blood circulation. There is a 13 percent reduction in retinal blood flow after caffeine intake,[4] so it's best to stay off the coffee and the colas.

Prolonged exposure to sunlight is another risk factor for macular degeneration, and the research in support of this is overwhelming. The more sun rays that reach the retina, the greater the risk of developing macular disease. One study found that those who were highly exposed to summer sun had double the rate of macular degeneration, while those who wore hats and sunglasses had 40 percent less than the normal rate.[5] In the tropics, retinal changes appeared in just four months in outdoor workers.

Most eye doctors today believe that sunlight is a major cause of macular degeneration and that everyone needs protection from ultraviolet light. Some even recommend reducing exposure to blue-violet light since the high energy in these photons can trigger toxic reactions in eye tissue. Wear a good pair of sunglasses that block out 100 percent of the UVA and UVB rays and filter out at least 85 percent of the blue-violet sun rays.

PREVENTION AND TREATMENT

Although conventional ophthalmologists offer no effective treatments for macular degeneration, it can be prevented, and, once diagnosed, can be treated with holistic treatments.

The Vision Diet

There are hundreds of research studies that show that what you eat has some effect on your macular health. Unfortunately, food alone can't provide maximally effective help. The levels of nutrients found in foods and in typical multivitamins have no significant impact on the progression of macular degeneration. The Vision Diet, outlined in Chapter 1, is a good place to start, but supplements are necessary too. Large doses of certain supplements not only have been shown to reduce the risk of macular degeneration, but they also have been shown to improve vision in people who already have the disease. This may be partially due to increased digestive powers and increased absorption of important vitamins, minerals and other nutrients. And since it can take up to nine months for retinal receptors to rejuvenate, any nutritional program for macular degeneration should be taken for a minimum of nine months.

Vitamins, Minerals, Amino Acids and Other Supplements

The following are some of the essential nutrients for treating macular degeneration. Other recommended nutrients can be found in the Macular Degeneration Prevention Program at the end of this chapter.

Beta-carotene. High blood levels of the antioxidants beta-carotene, selenium and vitamins C and E reduce the risk for macular degeneration. Beta-carotene, which protects against photosensitivity problems in the skin, may also protect the retina against photooxidative stress. Low blood levels of beta-carotene virtually double the risk for macular degeneration. Increasing one's intake of foods high in beta-carotene (deep orange and dark leafy green vegetables) can protect against macular degeneration.

Vitamin B2 (riboflavin). Riboflavin, which aids in the reception of light by the retina, is necessary for glutathione production. Taking just 10 mg of riboflavin per day increases glutathione by 83 percent.[6]

Vitamin B3 (niacin). Niacin dilates blood vessels, which allows for more nutrients and oxygen to reach the eye. Niacin also can help improve night blindness, which is often an early sign of metabolic stress in the retina.

Vitamin B6 (pyridoxine hydrochloride). Virtually all patients with wet macular degeneration are severely deficient in vitamin B6.

Biotin. Biotin improves vision in some cases of macular degeneration. It helps in the metabolism of essential fatty acids.

Vitamin C. The macula is the most metabolically active tissue in the body and produces the most free radicals. Antioxidants help prevent the damage done to the body by free radicals. The macula also is the body tissue most dependent on adequate circulation, not only to deliver oxygen, antioxidants and other nutrients, but to remove metabolic waste products as well. The queen of the antioxidants, vitamin C, helps in all these actions, plus it serves as a natural ultraviolet filter inside the eye, which may slow the natural retinal aging process. People with low blood levels of vitamin C have two to three times the risk for macular degeneration.

Vitamin E. Vitamin E stabilizes cell membranes, reduces the cell's need for oxygen, increases blood flow through atherosclerotic blood vessels, decreases leakage from blood vessels and provides antioxidant protection. People with low blood levels of vitamin E have double the risk for macular degeneration. The deficiency has been shown to cause macular degeneration in rats.

Amino acids. Two amino acids, *cysteine* and *taurine,* are important for a healthy retina. Cysteine, taken as N-acetyl-cysteine (NAC), increases production of glutathione, one of the most important antioxidants in the eye. Glutathione protects retinal cells from light damage caused by ultraviolet and blue light sunlight. Retinal cells grown *in vitro* without glutathione become weak, while those provided glutathione remain healthy. Macular degeneration patients have 58 percent less glutathione than people without the disease.[7] Glutathione deficiency can result from an imbalance in the intestinal bacterial flora.

Taurine is important for the maintenance of vision and the regeneration of worn out tissues of the visual system. It is found in high concentrations in the retina, especially in the photoreceptor cells, where it protects cells from ultraviolet damage. But it decreases with age. Studies have shown that when taurine is removed from food, animals develop retinal degeneration which is reversed upon the replacement of taurine. Taurine should be taken on an empty stomach.

Bioflavonoids. Bioflavonoids are neither vitamin nor mineral. Bioflavonoids such as *quercetin* and *rutin,* are plant pigments that help protect the eyes from sunlight damage. More than 4,000 plants contain bioflavonoids, but they are found in large amounts in red onions, cherries, red grapes and citrus fruits.

A specific type of bioflavonoid called *anthocyanidins* absorbs sunlight similar to melanin in the retina of the eye. Quercetin, with properties similar to melanin, protects the eye from damage by solar radiation and works synergistically with taurine and vitamin E. Rutin has been shown to reduce leakage from small blood vessels in the retina.

Garlic. Garlic helps prevent blood clots from forming in the small blood vessels of the retina.

Lutein and zeaxanthin. These two carotenoids are found in high levels in collard greens and spinach, and they appear to reduce the risk for macular degeneration, according to researchers at Harvard Medical School, who came to that conclusion after evaluating the diets of more than 800 eye patients. Eating these dark leafy vegetables at least once a week was enough to begin lowering risk; at a frequency of two to four times a week, the risk was lowered by 46 percent and was even greater at five to six times per week.[8]

Lutein and zeaxanthin supplements are best taken separately from beta-carotene supplements because they compete for absorption. Also, they need fat to absorb well, so take them with food or a small amount of olive oil.

Lycopene. Similar to lutein and zeaxanthin, lycopene also is neither vitamin nor mineral; it is a natural red pigment, a fat soluble antioxidant related to beta-carotene, but with twice the antioxidant power, making it ten times more powerful than vitamin E. It is found in high levels in tomato, guava, watermelon and pink grapefruit. People with a low dietary intake of lycopene have twice the risk of macular degeneration.

Selenium. Selenium makes sure that glutathione is doing its job. It does this so well that patients with macular degeneration have reported improved vision after taking selenium and vitamin E.

Zinc. Vision has been stabilized and even improved in people with macular degeneration who take zinc. Apparently, zinc is needed at higher concentrations in the eye than in most tissues, and the macula degenerates when zinc is deficient. Zinc levels in the retina also affect the level of melanin, which protects against photooxidative damage and is known to decrease after age 50.

Essential Fatty Acids

See Chapter 1 for general information regarding essential fatty acids (EFAs). In general, a very low-fat diet (10 percent of calories from fat) that excludes red meat and dairy products has been shown to reduce the risk of macular degeneration.[9] However, the lack of essential fatty acids, in the form of omega-3 oils, is also a risk factor. When treated with omega-3 fatty acids for four weeks, 85 percent of macular degeneration patients over age 70 experienced improved vision.[10]

A diet deficient in omega-3 fatty acids is known to cause impaired vision both in animals and in people.[11] Low birth weight infants deprived of omega-3 fats because they are not breastfed sometimes experience visual problems. But when EFAs are added to their formula, their visual acuity improves. Animal studies also show that, with age, omega-3 levels in the eye begin to fall. Omega-3 is so essential to the retina that, when this happens, it won't let go; the retina begins to recycle it within the eye.[12]

Apparently, omega-3 fats are essential for nerve conduction in the retina and to reduce cholesterol, thus helping to maintain retinal nutrition by keeping retinal blood vessels open. But one caution: the more omega-3 fats in the diet, the more antioxidant protection from vitamins C, E and beta-carotene is required.

The best sources of omega-3 EFAs are the flesh of cold water marine fish as well as black currant oil, flaxseed and flaxseed oil and hemp seed. We recommend that you either eat fish rich in omega-3 fats three times per week or take it as a supplement.

Omega-6 EFAs are also important to protect cells from degenerative changes and to reduce inflammation throughout the body. Sources of omega-6 fatty acids are evening primrose oil, borage oil and black currant oil.

Traditional Chinese Medicine

In Traditional Chinese Medicine, macular degeneration is seen primarily as a deficiency in the liver meridian with inefficient blood circulation. Both the kidney and the spleen meridians have also been found to be deficient.

The herbs and acupressure points prescribed for macular degeneration are chosen for their abilities to increase the qi in the liver, kidney and spleen meridians. They will harmonize the function of these organs and increase the smooth flow of energy and blood throughout the body, thus bringing increased circulation to the eyes.

Acupressure

See the Macular Degeneration Prevention Program, pages 86–87 for the acupressure points for macular degeneration.

Herbal Remedies

A combination of Chinese and Western herbs have been shown to improve the circulation of blood and energy to the eyes. The Chinese formula we use for macular degeneration is Hsiao Yao Wan (Relaxed Wanderer). This is the standard remedy for constrained energy in the liver meridian.

Hsiao Yao Wan helps the liver in its job of spreading qi throughout the body and to the eyes. The most important herb in this formula is bupleurum, whose primary role is to break through obstructions and restore the free flow of energy and blood. The adjunct herbs in the combination — peony root, dong quai, poria fungus, atractylodes, ginger, licorice — support the liver and digestive system. They help to relieve dampness, promote digestion and move and disperse stuck energy.

In addition to Hsiao Yao Wan, we recommend agrimony, bilberry, ginkgo biloba, ginseng (American and Siberian), milk thistle, dandelion and eyebright.

Agrimony (Agrimonia pilosa) is an astringent herb, meaning it can bind excess fluid, especially blood, so it is particularly good for patients whose macular degeneration involves subretinal bleeding.

Bilberry (Vaccinium myrtillus), the European version of the blueberry, has been called the vision herb for its powerful effect on all types of visual disorders. Research has shown that bilberry can improve night vision, relieve visual fatigue, and protect the eyes from glaucoma, cataracts and macular degeneration. Bilberry improves the delivery of oxygen and blood to the eyes, strengthens the capillaries that feed eye muscles and nerves, and works as an antioxidant to inhibit damage by free radicals.

Researchers believe that the flavonoids in bilberry called *anthocyanosides* can help prevent or even cure macular degeneration. As an antioxidant, bilberry can scavenge free radicals that can weaken blood vessel walls, causing them to leak. In addition, bilberry strengthens the collagen, which further improves the integrity of the blood vessels, reducing, and in some cases, preventing capillary leakage associated with the more serious wet form. Bilberry also has been shown to improve ocular circulation and oxygenation.

Currently, researchers at the Kellogg Eye Institute at the University of Michigan are conducting a clinical evaluation of bilberry and its effect in deterring and curing macular degeneration.

Ginkgo (Ginkgo biloba) has been shown to increase visual acuity in people with macular degeneration. As we have repeated many times throughout this book, ginkgo increases blood circulation to the head, which includes the brain and the eyes, so it can speed healing of all of the tissues associated with vision.

Ginseng (Panax ginseng) has been used traditionally as a tonic to support the effects of aging. A combination of American and Siberian ginseng help tonify the adrenal glands, a kidney function in Traditional Chinese Medicine. Macular degeneration benefits from strengthened kidneys, so ginseng can be helpful in this way.

Milk thistle (silybum marianum) is an excellent liver tonic. It increases the flow of bile from the liver, helping to detoxify poisons in our bloodstream. It nourishes the liver, reducing stress and increasing energy throughout the body.

Dandelion root (Taraxacum officinalis radix) is another universal liver tonic, aiding in digestion and balancing blood sugar levels, which combine to create good health for the eyes. In addition, dandelion contains antioxidants to help tissues stay healthy.

Eyebright (Euphrasis officinalis) has been known throughout history as an effective herb to help tonify the eyes.

Macular Degeneration Formula

In addition to the Hsiao Yao Wan formula mix one to two ounces of each of the other herb tinctures together and take one teaspoon twice a day for six to nine months. If the herbs are in capsule form, follow the directions of your health care practitioner. A formula combining most of these recommended herbs is available from Integral Health Apothecary or Starfire International (see Resources).

Homeopathic Remedies

The following remedies have been shown to be helpful for macular degeneration, but should *not* be taken without being evaluated by a qualified homeopath.

Phosphorus may be used for the "wet" type of macular degeneration which includes retinal bleeding.

Sepia is usually used for women who experience black spots in their vision accompanying macular degeneration.

Other Tips

- Because ultraviolet rays from sunlight cause so much damage to the eye, always wear protective sunglasses and hats when you are outside.

- Macular degeneration patients need reading light to be twice as bright as that found in the average home or office. Magnifiers help too.

- Aspirin thins the blood and increases blood flow to the retina; thus, it also can cause retinal hemorrhages. As a result, we *do not* recommend the use of aspirin for prevention of macular degeneration. However, bromelain, a mild blood thinner, can replace aspirin without its adverse retinal side effects.

CASE STUDIES

John

John DeCosta is a well-known radio personality in Hawaii with a wealth of knowledge and experience in the nutritional field. To his frustration, and despite a healthy diet and nutritional supplementation, he had progressed from the typical dry macular degeneration with small hard shiny deposits in the retina, and a loss of two lines of visual acuity over several years, to, at age 65, more serious wet macular degeneration with scarring, retinal bleeding and inflammation surrounding degenerating retinal drusen in the left eye.

Wet macular degeneration often affects one eye first and the other within several years. Visual acuity in the left eye had progressively dropped from 20/40 at the beginning of 1997 to 20/80, a disturbing 50 percent loss of vision, in a period of just six months. Very concerned about the rapid deterioration in John's vision, Harvard-trained retinal specialist Dr. Bruce Ballon immediately set up an emergency appointment for John to fly to Honolulu for laser cauterization of the leaking blood vessels. John, however, having had many positive experiences over the years with nutrition, elected to give natural vision care one last, but concerted effort to save his vision, knowing that the laser would certainly cause some additional damage to his retinal tissue.

John obtained a copy of Dr. Swartwout's summary of the nutritional literature on macular health and followed the recommendations carefully. He was already eating lots of fresh vegetables from his own garden, taking a good multivitamin and an antioxidant complex specifically designed for the eyes. He added eye drops containing vitamins A, C and E. To his daily supplement program he added bioflavonoids from pine, grape, bilberry and other sources. He also decided to add a small dose of ginkgo, avoiding higher doses because of the bleeding in his retina. He also increased his levels of carotenoids and vitamins B complex, C, D and E, as well as the minerals zinc picolinate and selenium. To this he added carnitine, N-acetyl-cysteine and MSM.

For years, John had also been taking an aspirin product containing caffeine for his headaches. When he learned that aspirin could contribute to his retinal bleeding, he stopped taking this product as part of his total healing program. He was pleased to find that after being on the whole regimen for four to five weeks, the headaches actually subsided.

At John's last checkup with Dr. Ballon, the noted retinologist was extremely pleased with John's response, stating that he had never seen such fast recovery in 12 years of practice. He reported that the retinal drusen were no longer swollen and decomposing. Not only had the bleeding, inflammatory and degenerative processes been halted completely, but to Dr. Ballon's amazement, even the retinal scarring was being reversed. In fact, John's remarkable improvement had made such an impression on him that Dr. Ballon described his case on a radio show several days later to illustrate the potential of our growing understanding of nutrition to heal the eyes and recover lost vision. John's vision had been fully restored to his previous level of 20/40.

Frances

Frances is a 78-year-old woman in good health. Her eye examination showed the following: right eye (with glasses) 20/50, left eye (with glasses) 20/70. These visual acuities were the same at both distance and near. Her main complaint was that when she tried to focus in on an object while reading or painting, the lines appeared wavy and fuzzy. She was getting depressed since she loved to read and paint. All of these visual tasks had become very frustrating. Her eye pressure was within normal range. She had been diagnosed with the "dry" type of macular degeneration by a conventional ophthalmologist, was told that it may stay the same or slowly worsen, and that there was nothing to be done for it except use a magnifier while reading and make sure she wore a hat and ultraviolet blocking sunglasses outdoors.

We explained to Frances that since macular degeneration is a progressive disease, there are many possible treatments to prevent it from worsening, and that these treatments might even improve her vision. After presenting her with the research, we recommended that she follow certain parts of the Macular Degeneration Prevention Program. After six months on this program, Frances' visual acuity in her right eye was 20/30; her left eye was 20/40. Not only was her vision improving, but she was less depressed and more excited about life.

NEW MEDICAL BREAKTHROUGHS FOR REVERSING MACULAR DEGENERATION[13]

Therapeutic Apheresis (Blood Cleansing and Purification)

This treatment is based on removing the toxic proteins and waste materials that "sludge up" the blood. This is done by removing high weight molecules from the blood, which then reduces damage to the capillary walls and allows a more active transport of nutrients and waste products to and from the macula. If enough cells are regenerated in the macula, vision improves. The procedure involves pumping an individual's blood through a machine that removes the plasma. A replacement fluid is added to maintain the correct volume of blood, and the blood is returned to the patient.

The effect of therapeutic apheresis usually lasts for a year. Since the procedure removes circulating and accumulated toxins, but does not stop their production, most patients will need one or two "booster" treatments every year after the initial treatment series. Each treatment can cost from $1,800 to $2,200 and takes 90 minutes.

Therapeutic apheresis has been used to treat neurological and chronic immune conditions safely for over 30 years. It is now considered one of the new promising treatments for age-related macular degeneration. For more information, contact Rheo Therapy Center at (888) 464-7436 or www.occulobix.com.

Fetal Cell Transplants

J. Terry Ernest, M.D., Ph.D., professor and chairman of the Department of Ophthalmology at the University of Chicago, is the first surgeon in the United States to transplant fetal retinal cells into an eye with macular degeneration. This is based on the theory that macular degeneration develops in the retinal pigment epithelium. These cells are necessary for the health of the retina. When these cells die, the part of the retina it supplies deteriorates. Therefore, transplantation of fetal retinal pigment cells to replace diseased ones can help produce new, healthy cells for the retina.

Thalidomide Treatment

Thalidomide, banned in the 1950s because it caused birth defects when taken during pregnancy, may be helpful in fighting macular degeneration.

New blood vessel growth (angiogenesis) is common in macular degeneration. This causes vessels to bleed and leak, thus causing reduced vision. Thalidomide may slow or block retinal vascular changes related to macular degeneration. As long as it is not taken during pregnancy, the drug seems to be relatively safe. Drug manufacturer EntreMed, Inc., is currently conducting clinical trials to investigate the efficacy of this experimental treatment.

Photodynamic Therapy

This is a treatment in which patients receive an intravenous infusion of a light-activated drug that collects in the tissues of the macula. A low-power laser light (664 nanometers) activates the drug and selectively destroys the abnormal vessels without damaging adjacent or overlying healthy tissue. Two light-activated drugs — Purlytin and Verteporfin — are now undergoing FDA clinical trials.

Photopoint, the photodynamic therapy that uses the drug Purlytin, was developed by Miravant Medical Technologies in partnership with Pharmacia and Upjohn. Iris Medical Instruments has conducted the clinical trials. Some patients have improved up to 4.5 lines on the eye chart after using this drug.

Verteporfin, developed by QLT Photo Therapeutics and Ciba Vision, demonstrated the ability to close abnormal leaking blood vessels without causing vision loss.

Electrical Stimulation

Since 50 percent of the blood passes through the eyes every 40 minutes, there is an opportunity to improve the blood supply to the retina with electricity applied from the cornea through the eye to the back of the head.

By using low direct current, the use of electrical stimulation has been shown to have some of the following benefits to the eye:

1. Attracts oxygen.

2. Prevents neurovascularization (an increase in the growth of new blood vessels).

3. Decreases hemorrhaging.

In a study of 65 patients with macular degeneration and other retinal diseases treated with light therapy, electrical stimulation and nutrition, 85 percent of the patients studied showed an improvement of at least one to four lines on the Snellen Eye Chart.[14]

MACULAR DEGENERATION PREVENTION PROGRAM

Vision Diet — *Follow the Vision Diet in Chapter 1 as closely as possible.*

- Beneficial foods include kale, raw spinach and collard greens, which have a high amount of lutein/zeaxanthin.
- Avoid refined sugars, coffee (and other caffeinated beverages), alcohol, margarine and red meat.
- Drink 8–10 glasses of water per day, but not with food — 30 minutes before a meal or 2 hours after a meal.

Nutritional Supplements — *Take the following vitamins and minerals on a daily basis:*

Beta-carotene	25,000 I.U.
Vitamin A	10,000 I.U.
Vitamin B1 (thiamin)	100 mg
B2 (riboflavin)	100 mg
B3 (niacin)	100 mg
B5 (pantothenic acid)	500 mg
B6 (pyroxidine)	100 mg
Folic acid	1,000 mcg
B12 (cobalamin)	100 mcg

Choline	100 mg
Inositol	100 mg
Biotin	500 mcg
Vitamin C	3,000 mg
Quercetin	2,000 mg
Rutin	300 mg
Vitamin D	200 I.U.
Vitamin E	800 I.U.
N-acetyl-cysteine (NAC)	1,000 mg
Alpha lipoic acid	200 mg
Magnesium	500 mg
Calcium	500 mg for men, 800 mg for women
Coenzyme Q10	100 mg
L-Carnitine	500 mg
Ginkgo biloba	240 mg
Zinc	30 mg
Lutein	20 mg
Zeaxanthin	300 mcg
Bilberry	300 mg
Omega-3 oils	1,500 mg
Omega-6 oils	1,500 mg
Selenium	200 mcg
Garlic	1,000 mg
Taurine	500 mg
Lycopene	20 mg

Acupressure Points

Massage each point for 30 seconds, twice a day:

1. Behind the Ball (*Qiuhou*)
2. Bladder 1 (*Jing Ming*)
3. Bladder 2 (*Zan Zhu*)
4. Gall Bladder 1 (*Tong Zi Liao*)
5. Gall Bladder 20 (*Feng Chi*)
6. Gall Bladder 37 (*Guang Ming*)
7. Kidney 3 (*Taixi*)
8. Large Intestine 4 (*Hoku*)

9. Liver 3 (*Tai Chang*)
10. Spleen 6 (*Sanyinjiao*)
11. Stomach 1 (*Cheng qi*)
12. Stomach 36 (*Zu San Li*)
13. *Tai Yang*
14. Triple Burner 23 (*Si Zhu Kong*)
15. *Yin Tang*
16. Bladder 18 (*Gan Shu*)
See the Appendix for the description and location of points.

Herbal Remedies
Take Hsiao Yao Wan (Relaxed Wanderer), 8 pills 3 times a day, or 12 pills twice a day; in tincture form, follow the instructions on the bottle. A tincture which combines agrimony, bilberry, ginkgo, ginseng, milk thistle, dandelion and eyebright is available from Integral Health Apothecary and Starfire International (see Resources). Take 1 teaspoon of this mixture twice a day.

Homeopathic Remedies
Consult a trained homeopath who can recommend the appropriate constitutional remedy for you with regard to your macular degeneration.

Medications
Avoid taking aspirin. Consult your physician for an alternative.

Exercises
Do 20 minutes of both aerobic and eye exercises at least four times per week (see Chapter 1).

Spinal Manipulation
Consult a qualified chiropractor or osteopath to make sure that the spine and neck are free from any energy blocks that might cause poor circulation and, thus, lack of energy to the eyes.

Eye Protection
Wear a hat and good ultraviolet-blocking sunglasses outdoors.

CHAPTER 5

Vision's Common Cold: Dry Eyes

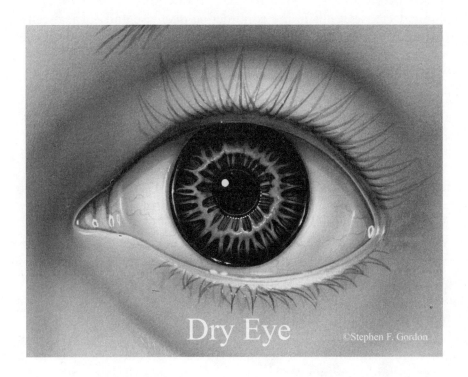

Dry Eye

©Stephen F. Gordon

The most frequent patient complaint to ophthalmologists and optometrists is dry eyes, known technically as *aqueous insufficiency*. About 33 million Americans in all age groups experience varying degrees of dry eye symptoms.[1] The symptoms may include dryness, grittiness, irritation, burning and even the seeming contradiction, of excessive tearing or watering.

Any condition that reduces the production, alters the composition or impedes the distribution of the tear film may result in dry eyes. Like most eye conditions, dry eye syndrome is often related to health conditions in the rest of the body. It is commonly associated with dryness of other mucous membranes, interior body surfaces such as joints and brittle nails. It also can be a sign of digestive imbalances or of more serious systemic autoimmune diseases, such as rheumatoid arthritis, Sjögren's syndrome or lupus erythematosus.

These diseases trigger an immune response, generating lymphocytes that slowly destroy the cells responsible for tear production and secretion. As a result, tear volume decreases, cells in the conjunctiva decrease and corneal cells can be lost, creating dry spots. In Sjögren's syndrome, for instance, the entire lacrimal gland — responsible for 90 percent of tear production — may be destroyed by the invasion of inflammatory lymphocytes.

WHO GETS DRY EYES?

Dry eyes are mostly a health problem for women, and seems to be a result of fluctuations in hormone levels, particularly estrogen and androgens. Pregnant women, women who use birth control pills and postmenopausal women on hormone replacement therapy frequently report dry eyes.

Dry eyes in postmenopausal women also can be a sign of Sjögren's syndrome, also known as Sicca syndrome. Sjögren's syndrome, which afflicts four million American women, is considered the most commonly misdiagnosed of all health conditions in women over the age of 40. In Sjögren's syndrome, dry eyes are accompanied by dryness in other parts of the body: dry mouth, dry joints (arthritis), sore throat, dry skin, dry cracked lips, dry scalp (dandruff) and brittle nails. This pattern of symptoms is produced by an autoimmune process in which antibodies attack fluid-secreting cells. Fatigue, Raynaud's disease and dental caries also are often present.

Dry eyes also can be an isolated problem. Older people naturally have drier eyes, because, as we get older, our eyes produce on average 40 percent less lubrication. Free radicals are partly to blame; they take their toll over time, damaging body tissues and increasing the prevalence of dry eye symptoms. Some people lack a sufficient volume of tears, or their tears might have the wrong composition. In addition, a problem with the eyelid can prevent the tears from distributing over the eyes properly.

Long-term contact lens use also can contribute to dry eyes, because, over time, contact lenses can reduce corneal sensitivity. The sensitivity of the cornea and the entire ocular surface determines how many tears the lacrimal gland will secrete. The less sensitive the cornea, the fewer tears you will have.

Forty percent of dry eye patients are smokers, so tobacco smoke, environmental allergens, air conditioning and wind may also cause dry eyes. Many medications trigger dry eye, most commonly antihistamines, codeine, decongestants, diuretics, morphine, oral contraceptives and even eye drops such as Visine and Murine.

WHAT ARE TEARS?

By understanding tears and tear production, we can find healthy solutions for many dry eye sufferers.

Tears are the clear, salty liquid that lubricates our eyes. There are actually three layers that keep the front surface of the eye comfortably lubricated and optically clear.

The outermost is an oily layer, secreted by the Meibomian glands *in the eyelids, that prevents the tears from evaporating and the eyelids from sticking together.*

The middle and thickest layer is the watery or aqueous layer, *which makes up about 90 percent of the tear film. This layer is secreted by the lacrimal glands, which formulate its secretions in small sac-like cells called* acinar cells. *Any damage to acinar cells reduces the lacrimal gland's ability to produce moisture. Many of the critical functions of the tear film — providing nutrients, removing debris, fighting bacteria and generally lubricating the eye — occur at this level.*

The innermost layer of the tear film, which binds the tears to the surface of the eye by making the eye tissue "wettable," is the mucous layer. This is secreted directly from the conjunctival surface *onto the white of the eye by the* goblet cells. *A breakdown in any one of these layers can cause dry eyes.*

TREATING DRY EYES

Standard medical treatment for dry eyes includes two options: artificial tear preparations in the form of eye drops or punctal occlusion.

Artificial Tears

Although many people find temporary relief with artificial tear preparations, they merely palliate the symptoms. Worse, the preservatives in many of these products can aggravate the condition. In fact, they can even kill corneal cells. Eye drops called *vasoconstrictors,* that promise to "get the red out," will reduce circulation in the eye, decrease production of the tear film, and worse, eventually make your eyes even drier.

Always use eye drops without preservatives. These have been shown to enhance corneal healing and improve dry eye problems.[2] A good brand is Thera Tears, which has been shown to aid in the healing of dry eyes after eight weeks of treatment. (Use two to six drops in each eye four times a day, at 8 a.m., noon, 3 p.m. and 6 p.m.; see Resources.)

Another good eye drop solution is Viva-Drops, which contains antioxidants and vitamin A. Patients have reported 90 percent improvement in several studies. Use two or three times a day for 30 days.

HOW TO USE EYE DROPS

Eye drops can be difficult to use, particularly for children and the elderly. Few doctors instruct their patients in using eye drops, so up to 80 percent of people have difficulty with this initially. Even with practice, 49 percent continue to have poor aim.[3]

Using eye drops is actually simple if you pull down the lower lid and let the eye drops fall into the lower lid rather than directly onto the cornea. (See illustration.)

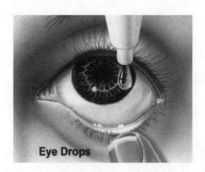

Eye Drops

If you can't seem to keep your eyes open while the drops fall into the eyes, drop them into the inner corner of the closed lids and the drop will enter the eyes on opening.

Blinking and tearing following use of eye drops can dilute them to less than one percent of their original concentration in just a few minutes. Therefore, don't blink, but rather close the eyes for up to two minutes to give the drops a chance to work.[4] Pinching gently at the bridge of the nose to prevent drainage through the tear ducts also will increase the effectiveness of the eye drops by 65 percent.[5] Other tips:

- *Wash your hands before using eye drops and keep the bottle in a clean place.*

- *If the eye drops sting your eyes, keep the eye drops refrigerated. The cold will lessen the sting.*

- *Be sure to keep your eye drops separate from any similar looking bottles. To prevent contamination, be careful not to touch the dropper with anything, including fingers or the eye itself. If there is a dirty ring between the cap and the lid, the eye drops probably are contaminated and should be discarded.*

Punctal Occlusion

Many patients tire of using eye drops and turn to punctal occlusion, which provides long-term relief.

Punctal occlusion is a procedure used to help dry eye patients. It is based on the theory that if the tear outflow is limited by occluding the area from which the tears flow, the amount of tears will increase so that the overall length of time that tears are in contact with the cornea will increase. This may help dry eye patients be more comfortable.

Punctal occlusion closes the drains that draw away excess fluids from the eyes. Here's how it works: There are tear drainage canals on the margins of the upper and lower eyelids near the nose. Inside the drainage opening are tiny pumps that suck away fluid from the surface of the eyes.

In punctal occlusion, the doctor closes the drains with silicone plugs, which keeps most of the fluids from being pumped away. In one study, 85 percent of patients with dry eyes were able to reduce their need for artificial tears to occasional use.[6]

PREVENTION AND TREATMENT

Holistic medical treatments can help alleviate dry eyes for many patients.

The Vision Diet

Follow the Vision Diet outlined in Chapter 1, making sure to eat lots of green leafy vegetables. One of the more important aspects of the Vision Diet for people who suffer from dry eyes is the prohibition against sugar and/or artificial sweeteners. Sugar increases the risk for dry eyes. Consumption of more than 11 teaspoons of sugar per day (most of which is hidden in processed foods) has been linked to dry eye syndrome. A single can of soda contains about nine teaspoons of sugar, and sugar is hidden throughout the processed and refined food kingdom in cereals, ketchup and salad dressings — in almost every processed food.

Avoid the toxic fats in commercial red meat, dairy products, fried foods and hydrogenated oils (such as margarine and shortening). These fats interfere with the proper metabolism of essential fatty acids in the body and are indirect causes of dry eye syndrome.

If you suffer from Sjögren's syndrome, you are deficient in gastric acids, particularly hydrochloric acid and pepsin. Acidophilus, bifidus and other friendly bacterial flora supplements are recommended to improve the function of the gastrointestinal tract. We recommend about six billion viable organisms (in a *probiotic* supplement) three times a day.

Vitamins and Minerals

The following are some of the essential nutrients for treating dry eyes. Other recommended nutrients can be found in the Dry Eyes Prevention Program at the end of this chapter.

Vitamin A. In parts of the world where vitamin A deficiency is widespread, severe dry eye syndrome is a leading cause of blindness. Vitamin A is needed for the health of all epithelial (surface) tissues; it is actually found in the tear film of healthy eyes, and it is fundamental to the production of the mucous layer of the tears.

We recommend eye drops containing vitamin A and vitamin C because they protect the eyes from free radicals, such as toxins, irritants, allergens and inflammation. In addition, take a daily oral dose of 10,000 I.U. of vitamin A and 25,000 I.U. of beta-carotene (also called provitamin A because it converts to vitamin A in the body).

Note: Before beginning a regimen of vitamin A or beta-carotene, have your thyroid activity checked by your health care practitioner. Hypothyroid patients — people with underactive thyroids — are always vitamin A deficient. They cannot convert beta-carotene to vitamin A, nor can they convert vitamin A to the form usable by the eyes. One way to check this yourself is to take your temperature under your arm when you wake up in the morning, but before you get out of bed. If it is regularly below 97.8°F, you might have an underactive thyroid (see page 6).

Vitamin B6. All of the B vitamins are important in treating dry eyes, but vitamin B6, also called pyridoxine, aids in the proper absorption of magnesium. Magnesium helps the body produce a hormone called *prostaglandin E-7,* which is necessary for tear production.

Folic acid. Another B vitamin, folic acid, also called folacin and folate, is directly responsible for the level of potassium in the body and potassium is critical for fluid metabolism.

Vitamin C. Vitamin C is concentrated in the tear film to a higher level than that found in the blood. As we discussed earlier, it protects the eyes from free radicals, such as toxins, irritants, allergens and inflammation. Vitamin C is also needed for proper sugar metabolism.

Vitamin E. Vitamin E along with other nutrients are helpful for dry eye patients.

Potassium. Probably the most important intracellular mineral for dry eye symptoms, potassium is usually very low in dry eye patients. This is usually linked to low intakes of folic acid, vitamin C and vitamin B6 along with high sugar consumption. You can take in at least 500 mg per day by increasing your consumption of fresh fruits and vegetables (one banana, for example, contains 400 mg).

Other minerals. A person with Sjögren's syndrome usually lacks the ability to absorb minerals, particularly calcium, magnesium and zinc. These minerals, plus sodium, are essential for healthy tear film, as well as a healthy cornea.

Essential Fatty Acids

Dry eye sufferers also might want to consider supplementing their diets with essential fatty acids (see Chapter 1). Essential fatty acids (EFAs) are just that — essential — for the production of both the oily, lipid layer and the watery, aqueous layer of tear film.

After only about ten days of taking EFAs in the form of evening primrose oil, plus vitamins B6 and C, dry eye sufferers have seen an increase in tear production.[7,8] In another study, tear production almost doubled in the first month among dry eye patients taking 3,000 mg of evening primrose oil, 25 to 50 mg of vitamin B6 and 1,500 mg of vitamin C.

Traditional Chinese Medicine

In Traditional Chinese Medicine, we view dry eyes as a deficiency in the kidney and liver meridians. The flow of tears is controlled by the liver, and the kidneys (water element) play an important role in whether or not dryness is present anywhere in the body. The herbs and acupressure points prescribed for dry eyes are chosen for their abilities to increase tear flow and tear production in the eyes.

Acupressure

The acupressure points which have long been used in the traditional treatment of dry eye syndrome are listed in the Dry Eye Prevention Program, page 102.

Herbal Remedies

We have found that a combination of Chinese and Western herbs is effective for the treatment of dry eyes. The Chinese formula is called Lycii-Rehmannia. The herbs included are rehmannia root, cornus fruit, dioscorea root, alisma root, poria fungus, moutan, lycium berry and chrysanthemum flowers. This combination is a classic tonic for visual problems associated with a yin deficient condition. (In Chinese medicine, yin deficient syndromes involve a dry and/or hot situation, such as dry, irritated and/or itchy eyes or photophobia.)

We add ginkgo, American ginseng and licorice to this formula, and in case of hormonal imbalance, damiana and vitex.

Ginkgo (Ginkgo biloba) has a long respected history of use throughout time in cultures worldwide. It has been shown to increase and support the circulation of blood to the head, including the eyes as well as the brain. In this way, it promotes rapid healing of all the tissues associated with vision.

American Ginseng (Panax quinquefolium) is a wonderful general overall tonic for the body. Like the Asian and Siberian ginsengs, it has been shown to have an adaptogenic or balancing effect on adrenal function. But whereas the Asian varieties seem to support the qi and the yang, American ginseng is gentler and has more of a yin supportive function. This herb supports immune function, counteracts fatigue and balances blood sugar levels (which indirectly support the eyes).

Licorice (Glycyrrhiza glabra) is a moistening and tonifying herb. Traditionally used in Chinese medicine as a "unifying" herb, it helps bring out and harmonize the actions of other herbs. Plus, licorice has been shown repeatedly to support and balance adrenal function; therefore, it can be an important anti-inflammatory agent.

Herbs that regulate hormone levels may help people with dry eye syndrome because tear production and the function of the Meibomian or tarsal glands (oil glands that help prevent the eyelids from sticking together) are dependent on systemic hormone levels. Androgens and progesterone, for example, seem to be key for the proper functioning of the lacrimal glands.

Logically, then, herbs that help regulate these hormones could improve dry eye symptoms (for example, for postmenopausal women). These herbs include:

Damiana (Turnesa aphrodisiaca or diffusa) strengthens the hormonal system and contains an alkaloid that acts like testosterone.

Vitex (Agnus castus), known also as chaste tree berry or chasteberry, stimulates the production of progesterone.

Homeopathic Remedies

Homeopathic remedies are most effective when they are prescribed on an individualized basis, taking into account the condition of the whole patient, not just one symptom or another. We recommend consulting a qualified homeopath if the following remedies do not help.

We generally prescribe four remedies for patients with dry eyes: Silicea, Euphrasia, Apis and Similisan #1 (or #2 if allergic).

Silicea 6C is prescribed if the person is experiencing excessive watering of the eyes, which may be due to a lack of mucin or to a blocked tear duct. This leads to dry spots that stimulate nerve reflexes to produce more tears in an attempt to rewet the cornea, which contains more nerve endings per square millimeter than any other part of the body.

Euphrasia is prescribed when the eyes tend to water with a burning sensation or if they feel very dry (as if there is sand in them). The lids may also be red.

Apis is prescribed when the eyes feel very dry and hot. In this case, the tearing will also feel hot and the eyes will be red.

Similisan (homeopathic eye drops) are available in two forms — for those with dry eyes: Similisan #1 containing Belladonna 6x, Euphrasia 6x, and Mercuris 6x; and Similisan #2, containing Apis 6x, Euphrasia 6x, and Sabidilla 6x, for allergic irritation.

Emotions and Dry Eyes

See Chapter 1 for general information on emotional health as it relates to your eyes. One researcher found that the level of a stress chemical found in tears (called *prolactin*) may play a role in determining whether dry eyes will develop. When prolactin levels drop after menopause, women sometimes suffer from dry eye syndrome. Drugs that retard prolactin production have also been found to produce dry eye syndrome.

CASE STUDY

Betty P. was a 62-year-old woman complaining of dry eyes. Her visual acuity without glasses was 20/20 right eye, 20/20 left eye. For near vision she needed glasses of a prescription of +2.50 in each eye. Her ocular health was within normal limits. There was no evidence of cataracts. Her intraocular pressures were both normal. Her optic disk was within normal limits in both eyes. Six months before, she had seen another eye doctor, who had prescribed artificial tears. She said that the drops felt good when she put them in but within 15 minutes, her eyes were dry again. He spoke of the possibility of punctal occlusion but she decided against it.

Our approach began by unraveling the underlying causes of the dryness. We examined her diet, nutritional and hormonal status and considered supplements, herbs and homeopathy.

Her diet generally consisted of red meat once a week and chicken or turkey two to three times a week. She ate fruits and vegetables approximately four times a week. She drank one or two cups of coffee per day. She ate dessert with her dinner and lunch every day. She said her eyes usually became very dry about 30 minutes after meals. She did not smoke and drank alcohol very occasionally. When she did drink red wine, she felt her cheeks flush. She ate fried foods occasionally and used margarine on her toast approximately three to four times a week.

At the time of the visit, she was taking 1,000 mg of vitamin C a day and 400 I.U. of vitamin E.

Betty's blood pressure was normal, and she had no evidence of diabetes, heart disease or thyroid problems. She was susceptible to sore throats, her lips were dry, and her nails were dry and brittle. Her estrogen levels were low.

We advised Betty to follow parts of the Dry Eye Prevention Program. After following this protocol for one month, Betty reported over a 75 percent improvement in her dry eyes, with a definite increase in tear flow.

DRY EYES PREVENTION PROGRAM

Vision Diet   *Follow the Vision Diet in Chapter 1 as closely as possible.*

- Beneficial foods include fresh fruits (especially bananas and green leafy vegetables, such as kale and collard greens) along with cold water fish like salmon, mackerel and sardines.
- Avoid refined sugars, artificial sweeteners, alcohol, fried foods, dairy products, non-organic red meat and hydrogenated oils (margarine and shortening). Drink 8–10 glasses of water per day, but not with food — 30 minutes before a meal or 2 hours after a meal.

Nutritional   *Take the following vitamins and minerals on a daily*
Supplements   *basis:*

Vitamin A	10,000 I.U.
Beta-carotene	15,000–25,000 I.U.
Vitamin B1 (thiamin)	100 mg
B2 (riboflavin)	100 mg
B3 (niacin)	100 mg
B5 (pantothenic acid)	500 mg
B6 (pyroxidine)	100 mg
Folic acid	1,000 mcg
B12 (cobalamin)	100 mcg
Choline	100 mg
Inositol	100 mg
Biotin	500 mcg
Vitamin C (buffered form)	3,000 mg
Vitamin D	200 I.U.
Vitamin E	800 I.U.
Chromium	200 mcg
Selenium	200 mcg
Calcium	500 mg for men, 800 mg for women
Magnesium	500 mg

Omega-3 oils	3,000 I.U.
Omega-6 oils	1,500 I.U.
Quercetin	2,000 mg
Rutin	300 mg
Zinc	30 mg
Potassium	500 mg

Acupressure Points

Massage each point for 30 seconds, twice a day:

1. Bladder 1 (*Jing Ming*)
2. Gall Bladder 1 (*Tong Zi Liao*)
3. Gall Bladder 14 (*Yangbai*)
4. Kidney 6 (*Zhaohai*)
5. Large Intestine 4 (*Hoku*)
6. Liver 8 (*Ququan*)
7. Stomach 1 (*Cheng Qi*)
8. Stomach 36 (*Zu San Li*)
9. Bladder 23 (*Shen Shu*)

See the Appendix, pp. 131–38 for the description and location of points.

Herbal Remedies

Take a combination of Lycii-Rehmannia along with ginkgo biloba, American ginseng and licorice — available from Integral Health Apothecary and Starfire International (see Resources). Take either 1 teaspoon of the above combination in tincture form twice per day without food, or if in capsule/pill form, follow the directions on the label or from your health care practitioner.

If you are experiencing postmenopausal or other hormonal imbalance symptoms as well, add a teaspoon each of damiana and vitex twice a day.

Homeopathic Remedies

Consult a trained homeopath who can recommend the appropriate constitutional remedy for you with regard to your dry eyes.

Medications	Recommended eye drops are Thera Tears, Similisan #1 (#2 for allergic irritations) or Viva eye drops (see Resources). Follow instructions on label for frequency of application.
Exercises	Do 20 minutes of both aerobic and eye exercises at least four times per week (see Chapter 1).
Spinal Manipulation	Consult a qualified chiropractor or osteopath to make sure that the spine and neck are free from any energy blocks that might cause poor circulation and, thus, lack of energy to the eyes.
Emotional Health	Decrease stress from your life. Try meditation, yoga, tai chi, biofeedback techniques, qi gong or psychotherapy.

Chapter 6

Sties

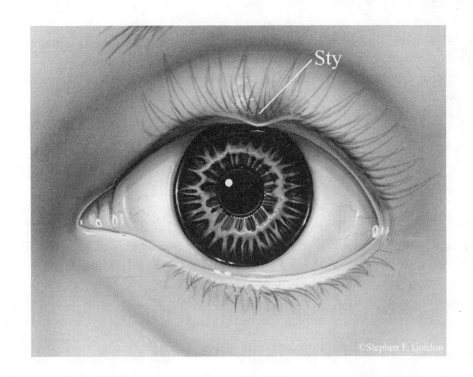

The common sty is simply an infection or inflammation of one of the oil or sebaceous glands that lies along the edge of the eyelid. Sties appear as painful red lumps and then develop heads of whitish pus. Usually some unnoticed chronic infection of the eyelid is the cause. They are not contagious and cannot be passed from person to person.

Children tend to develop sties more often than adults, probably because children's glandular secretions are more erratic, especially during puberty, and children tend to be less careful about keeping their hands clean and away from their eyes.

CONVENTIONAL TREATMENT

When treatment is begun early — right after a sty is first noticed — it will usually clear up in a couple of days. Sties are usually treated with plain hot compresses, although you could also use a boric acid solution. Many doctors prescribe antibiotic drops or ointment to control the infection. Sties rarely require excision, and under no circumstances should a sty be squeezed — the eyelid is the thinnest skin on the body and is easily damaged.

HOLISTIC TREATMENT AND PREVENTION

The Vision Diet

There is often a relationship between a patient's diet and digestive system and diseases of the eyelid. Poor digestion and improper diet (such as fried foods) often can cause problems such as sties. If this is the case, the onset of the sty is typically more gradual.

If you are prone to sties, reduce your intake of saturated fat and avoid hydrogenated oils and fried foods. Take 1,500 mg of essential fatty acids (EFAs) per day such as flaxseed, borage and/or evening primrose oils. (See Chapter 1 for more information on EFAs.) In addition, to maintain overall health and circulation, take a good multi-mineral vitamin containing the nutrients recommended in the Sty Prevention Program at the end of this chapter.

Traditional Chinese Medicine

In Traditional Chinese Medicine, sties are considered the result of an external infection generated by the environment or as an internal imbalance from a dysfunction of the spleen and stomach meridians. When the spleen and stomach are not working properly, the ability of the body to transport fluids in the eyes stagnates, and sties may occur.

The herbs and acupressure points prescribed for sties were chosen for two reasons: 1) for their ability to improve the smooth functioning of the spleen energy, thereby improving the flow of fluids through the eyelids; 2) to increase the immunity of the body so that it is less vulnerable to infection from the outside environment.

Acupressure

Refer to the Sty Prevention Program at the end of this chapter for the acupressure points that are helpful in alleviating sties.

Herbal Remedies

The following herbs are helpful in the treatment of sties:

Burdock root (Arctium lappa) is a liver tonic and lymphatic cleanser. Herbalists have traditionally used burdock for skin conditions, such as sties, boils and carbuncles.

Echinacea (Echinacea angustifolia) is one of the most popular immune boosters. It not only supports the body's ability to fight its own battles by enhancing our immune response, but it also has its own antibacterial and antiseptic qualities.

Forsythia (Forsythia suspensa), recognized in Traditional Chinese Medicine as a "cooling" herb, has been shown to inhibit viral and bacterial infections, including staphylococcus, streptococcus and salmonella.

Goldenseal (Hydrastis canadensis) is gaining popularity for its natural yet potent antibiotic and antiseptic qualities. American herbalists have prescribed it for more than 100 years to treat inflammation of the eyes.

Honeysuckle (Lonicerae japonicae), like forsythia, clears the "heat" of infection and inflammation and alleviates the swelling of sties. A natural antibiotic, it has been shown to inhibit viral and bacterial infections, including staphylococcus, streptococcus and salmonella.

Chrysanthemum flower (Chrysanthemum marifoli) is used in the treatment of many eye conditions for its antibiotic effect. It is useful in relieving heat in the eyes, such as in the conditions of sties and conjunctivitis.

Eyebright (Euphrasia officinalis) has been known since the Middle Ages as a universal eye remedy for both internal and external inflammatory conditions.

Chamomile (Matricaria chamomilla) is a very effective herb when used externally as a compress to help with inflammatory conditions of the eye.

Red raspberry leaf (Rubus idaeus) is an astringent herb that helps to break up excess mucous in the eyes.

Calendula (Calendula officinalis) is a very effective herb in the treatment of inflammatory conditions when used externally. (Taken internally it aids digestion.)

Herbal Formula for Sties

Combine one to two ounces of tinctures of burdock, echinacea, forsythia, goldenseal, honeysuckle, chrysanthemum flower, eyebright, chamomile, red raspberry leaf and calendula. Take one teaspoon twice a day for two weeks. Also apply a compress to the sty using a tea made from any of these herbs, two to three times a day. This combination of herbs is also available from Integral Health Apothecary and Starfire International (see Resources).

Calendula and hypericum, if used together in a hot compress for ten minutes every two to three hours, help to draw the toxins out. They possess excellent antibacterial and antiviral properties.

HOW TO MAKE A COMPRESS

Make an herbal tea by adding two teaspoons of dried herbs or one-half dropperful of herbal tincture to one cup boiling water. Cover and let cool for 5–10 minutes. Soak a clean cloth in the (strained) warm tea, wring out and apply to your eyes. Leave until compress cools; repeat as often as desired, keeping the tea warm.

Homeopathic Remedies

Even though sties seem to be more of an external (surface-based) condition, they may be a sign of an underlying constitutional imbalance in the individual. Therefore, we recommend that you not only try the following remedies, but that you consult a qualified homeopath.

The following homeopathic remedies may be helpful in the treatment of sties.

Euphrasia is also helpful in treating sties as it helps with the drainage of the sinuses and clears the mucous membranes around the eyes.

Staphysagria is a good remedy to try for someone who experiences recurrent sties, typically at the area of the eyelid closer to the nose (inner canthus). There might also be itching at the margin of the eyelid, combined with dark circles under the eyes.

Belladonna can be tried at the first sign of a red, puffy eyelid.

Pulsatilla helps to relieve itching eyes with inflamed lids and sties.

Mercuris should be considered when a whitehead or scales around the eyes are present.

STY PREVENTION PROGRAM

Vision Diet

Follow the Vision Diet in Chapter 1 as closely as possible.

- If possible, fasting and/or a liver cleanse (see page 112) is recommended to help detoxify the body and the eyes.
- Avoid refined sugars, artificial sweeteners, alcohol, fried foods and non-organic red meat.
- Drink 8–10 glasses of water per day, but not with food — 30 minutes before a meal or 2 hours after a meal.

Nutritional Supplements

Take the following vitamin and mineral supplements on a daily basis:

Vitamin A	5,000–10,000 I.U.
Beta-carotene	10,000–25,000 I.U.
Vitamin B1 (thiamin)	100 mg
B2 (riboflavin)	100 mg
B3 (niacin)	100 mg
B5 (pantothenic acid)	500 mg
B6 (pyroxidine)	100 mg
Folic acid	1,000 mcg
B12 (cobalamin)	100 mcg
Choline	100 mg
Inositol	100 mg
Biotin	500 mcg
Vitamin C	1,500 mg (buffered form)
Vitamin D	200 I.U.
Vitamin E	400–800 I.U.
Zinc	30 mg
Chromium	200 mcg
Selenium	200 mcg
Calcium	500 mg for men, 800 mg for women
Magnesium	500 mg
Quercetin	2,000 mg
Rutin	300 mg

	Omega-3 oils	1,500 mg
	Omega-6 oils	1,500 mg

Acupressure Points — *Massage each point for 30 seconds, twice a day:*

1. Bladder 1 (*Jing Ming*)
2. Gall Bladder 1 (*Tong Zi Liao*)
3. Stomach 44 (*Neiting*)
4. Triple Burner 17 (*Yifeng*)
5. Bladder 10 (*Tian Zhu*)

See the Appendix, pp. 131–38 for the description and location of points.

Herbal Remedies — Take a teaspoon internally and apply a warm compress externally twice a day of the following combination of herbs: burdock, echinacea, forsythia, goldenseal, honeysuckle, chrysanthemum flower, eyebright, chamomile, red raspberry leaf and calendula. This combination is available through the Integral Health Apothecary and Starfire International (see Resources).

Homeopathic Remedies — Consult a trained homeopath who can recommend the appropriate constitutional remedy for you.

Medications — If, after one month of the Sty Prevention Program, there is no improvement, contact your physician to consider medication.

Exercises — Do 20 minutes of both aerobic and eye exercises at least four times per week (see Chapter 1).

Spinal Manipulation — Consult a qualified chiropractor or osteopath to make sure that the spine and neck are free from any energy blocks that might cause poor circulation and, thus, lack of energy to the eyes.

HOW TO DO A LIVER CLEANSE

Days 1 and 2
Eliminate all foods except fruits and vegetables. Consume fruits and vegetables in any form: steamed, sautéed, raw, juiced. Eat as much and as often as you like. If any oil is used, use olive oil.

Day 3
Drink only juices and water. Any and all fruit and vegetable juices are fine. Drink as much as you like, but take in no solid food.

Day 4
Drink only water and lemonade (see recipe below). Drink as much and as often as you like, but be sure to consume at least four 8-oz. glasses of lemonade in the course of the day. Before bedtime, take a tablespoon of pure virgin olive oil.

Day 5
Same as Day 3.

Days 6 and 7
Same as Days 1 and 2.

On all days of this cleanse, try to drink a minimum of eight 8-oz. glasses of water, preferably spring or distilled water. Twice a day, take a teaspoon of bulk fiber made from psyllium powder (available at any health food store).

Lemonade

2 Tbs. fresh-squeezed lemon juice, 1 Tbs. pure maple syrup (if desired), dash of cayenne pepper, 8 oz. of distilled or spring water.

CHAPTER 7

Floaters:
Out, Damned Spots!

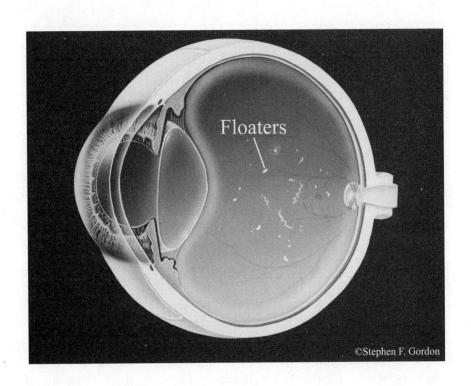

Floaters

©Stephen F. Gordon

Do tiny black shapes dance on your white living room wall? Do you catch little black circles or cones floating in your peripheral vision? Spots before the eyes, called floaters, can be frustrating to patients and doctors alike. The standard answer, once a serious physical problem has been ruled out, has been to learn to live with them.

Floaters are an appropriate name for these small dark shapes that appear before your eyes, because float through your field of vision is precisely what they do. These spots may look like dots, squiggles, strands or any of a hundred other shapes. Though they can be annoying, floaters are harmless, and there are ways to minimize or prevent them through proper diet and other methods discussed below. But if you suddenly become aware of floaters, of if they're accompanied by bright flashes of light, it could signal a retinal detachment and the need for emergency care.

> **Warning:** If you suddenly become aware of new spots in your vision, see your eye doctor right away to rule out serious problems.

WHAT CAUSES FLOATERS?

Generally, floaters are caused when cells or proteins in the vitreous humor stick or group together. Some also are remnants of fetal eye formation: as the eye develops before birth, blood vessels grow through the center of the eye. These blood vessels usually dissolve during the last three months before birth. Sometimes, however, they don't disappear completely, so those tiny "strands" you might see floating up the wall are actually shadows of those prenatal blood vessels.

Floaters also result when the vitreous becomes detached from its connection to the optic nerve. The tissue that attaches the vitreous to the optic nerve contains pigment in the shape of a ring, so when this detaches and floats in front of the retina, it casts an intense and disturbing shadow. About one-fourth of all Americans experience vitreous detachment; fortunately, there's usually no bleeding or retinal detachment.

Floaters are commonly found in nearsighted people and in people with food allergies and candidiasis. Vitreous detachment also is common in diabetics. But the highest rate of complaints of floaters is among people over age 70; this is when the prevalence of vitreous detachment jumps from 10 percent of the population to 63 percent.[1]

TREATMENT AND PREVENTION PROGRAM

The Vision Diet

The Vision Diet in Chapter 1 can help reduce congestion in the liver and colon, with the following guidelines:

1. For protein, emphasize fish, soy (in moderation), almonds, sunflower seeds and sesame seeds. Avoid meat, poultry, eggs, dairy products and most other nuts.

2. Eat brown rice and other whole grains instead of refined and processed grains (such as white bread and pasta).

3. Use unsulfured molasses and fruit juices for sweetening instead of white sugar, chocolate or honey.

4. Drink rice, almond or soy milk, herb teas or unsweetened, diluted fruit juices instead of coffee, tea, alcohol and dairy drinks.

5. Steam or bake foods instead of frying them.

6. Eat lots of vegetables, but avoid the nightshade family (e.g., tomatoes, green peppers, white potatoes and eggplant).

7. Eat less fruit in general, particularly citrus fruit, and select pineapple, melon and grapes.

8. Minimize your use of salt.

Vitamins and Minerals

The following are some of the essential nutrients for treating floaters. Other recommended nutrients can be found in the Floater Prevention Program at the end of this chapter.

Antioxidants, such as vitamins A, C and E, beta carotene, selenium and bioflavonoids may prevent damage to the vitreous, which causes floaters.

Vitamin C. Vitamin C not only strengthens the connective tissues in the eye, but it also concentrates in the vitreous, where it is found in higher levels than in any other tissues of the body. Take no more than 1,500 mg of vitamin C (buffered form, ascorbic acid) per day if you have floaters.[2] More than that may reduce the absorption of minerals such as calcium, chromium and copper, and actually result in vitreous damage.

Calcium. Calcium helps strengthen the eye's connective tissue. A low level of calcium in the blood, in proportion to phosphorus, has been related to an increase in nearsightedness and floaters.

Chromium. Chromium helps regulate blood sugar, circulation and fat metabolism, and helps prevent nearsightedness, a risk factor for vitreous degeneration and floaters. A lack of chromium can increase your risk for floaters eight-fold.

Copper. Copper is necessary for the antioxidant enzyme, superoxide dismutase, which protects the vitreous from the harmful effects of ultraviolet light.

Glucosamine sulfate. Glucosamine repairs and rebuilds the vitreous connective tissues.

Manganese. This mineral helps with allergies and blood sugar problems.

N-acetyl-cysteine (NAC) and *alpha lipoic acid* help to repair connective tissue.

Phosphorus. Calcium and phosphorus work together to maintain the body's proper acid balance. When this balance is not maintained, your risk for floaters increases. Because the American diet is typically high in phosphorus (due primarily to our high intake of soda and meat), avoid excess phosphorus.

Traditional Chinese Medicine

In Traditional Chinese Medicine, floaters are an indication of congestion in the liver, kidney and colon. The herbs and acupressure points prescribed for floaters are chosen for their abilities to eliminate congestion in these organs in order to keep the vitreous of the eye clear from these annoying specks.

Acupressure

See the Floater Prevention Program at the end of this chapter for the acupressure points that have long been used in the traditional treatment of vision problems.

Herbal Remedies

The herbs used in Chinese medicine for floaters harmonize the functions of the liver and support its ability to promote the smooth flow of energy, blood and emotions throughout the body, mind and spirit. They nourish the blood in the liver meridian (to help move that stuck qi) and strengthen the spleen and stomach. All of these combine to help resolve the congealing of fluid in the body (floaters are usually the literal reflections of congealed fluid in the eye). Our research has shown that a combination of Chinese, Western and Ayurvedic herbs are helpful in the treatment of floaters. We recommend the following herbs.

Hsiao Yao Wan (Relaxed Wanderer Pills) is the standard remedy for constrained energy in the liver meridian. These herbs help the liver to spread qi throughout the body and to the eyes. The most important herb in this formula is bupleurum, whose primary role it is to break through obstructions and restore the free flow of energy and blood. The adjunct herbs in this formula — peony root, dong quai, poria fungus, atractylodes, ginger and licorice — support the liver and digestive system. They help relieve dampness, promote digestion, and move and disperse stuck energy, thus helping the congealed fluid that composes floaters to disperse.

In addition to the Chinese formula, we add the following herbs:

Horsetail (Equisetum arvense) has the active constituent silica, which helps to repair connective tissue in the body and eye.

Ginkgo (Ginkgo biloba) promotes circulation and blood flow to the body and the eyes.

Milk thistle (Silybum marianum) is a powerful liver tonic that helps to purify the bloodstream.

Dandelion root (Taraxacum officinalis radix) is also a liver tonic that aids in digestion and balances blood sugar levels in the body.

A combination of these herbs will bring an increase of qi to the eyes in an effort to eliminate the congealed fluids or floaters. All herbs are available through Integral Health Apothecary and Starfire International (see Resources).

Homeopathic Remedies

Arnica montana, Carbo vegetabilis and *Lycopodium elevatum* have been shown to be helpful for floaters, but we recommend that you be evaluated by a qualified homeopath to address any underlying constitutional imbalance for which floaters may be just one symptom.

Wear Sunglasses

Invest in a pair of ultraviolet-filtering lenses. Ultraviolet light causes shrinkage, degeneration, liquification and clumping of proteins in the eye, and those clumps are what become floaters. Wearing these sunglasses is an especially important part of eye care for older people because vitreous detachments become more common as we age.

CASE STUDY

Paul C., 42, complained of very annoying, thread-like spots floating in front of his eyes. He had been examined by a conventional eye doctor, who, after determining that Paul's eyes were otherwise healthy, told him there was nothing that could be done for the floaters. "You're just going to have to get used to them," he told Paul. But Paul couldn't, and was determined to find a way to at least lessen them, so he sought a second opinion.

Paul is moderately nearsighted in both eyes. His visual acuity with glasses is 20/20 at a distance and near. His ocular health and retina are normal, he has no cataracts and his eye pressure is normal. We found floating clumps of protein in both eyes, the right eye slightly worse than the left.

We recommended certain parts of our Floater Prevention Program. Following this protocol, Paul's floaters lessened by about 50 percent over a period of six months.

Floater Prevention Program

Vision Diet   *Follow the Vision Diet in Chapter 1 as closely as possible.*

- Beneficial foods include fresh fruits (especially pineapple, apples and pears) and vegetables (especially carrots and spinach). Almonds, sunflower seeds and plain yogurt are also recommended.
- Avoid refined sugars, artificial sweeteners, other dairy products, nightshade vegetables (eggplant, peppers, tomatoes, white potatoes) and excess salt.
- Drink 8–10 glasses of water per day, but not with meals — 30 minutes before or 2 hours after a meal.

Nutritional Supplements   *Take the following vitamins and minerals on a daily basis:*

Vitamin A	10,000 I.U.
Beta-carotene	25,000 I.U.
Vitamin B1 (thiamin)	100 mg
B2 (riboflavin)	100 mg
B3 (niacin)	100 mg
B5 (pantothenic acid)	500 mg
B6 (pyroxidine)	100 mg
Folic acid	1,000 mcg
B12 (cobalamin)	100 mcg
Choline	100 mg
Inositol	100 mg
Biotin	500 mcg
Vitamin C	1,500 mg
Vitamin D	200 I.U.
Vitamin E	400 I.U.
Omega-3 oils	1,500 mg
Omega-6 oils	1,500 mg
Quercetin	2,000 mg
Rutin	300 mg

Bilberry	300 mg
Ginkgo biloba (24% extract)	160 mg*
Calcium	500 mg for men, 800 mg for women
Magnesium	500 mg
Chromium	200 mcg
Copper	2 mg
Manganese	20 mg
Selenium	200 mcg
Zinc	30 mg
N-acetyl-cysteine (NAC)	1,000 mg
Glucosamine sulfate	1,500 mg
Vanadium	200 mcg
Alpha lipoic acid	200 mg

*Take 40 mg if you are taking any blood thinner medication.

Acupressure Points

Massage each point for 30 seconds, twice a day:

1. Bladder 1 (*Jing Ming*)
2. *Tai Yang*
3. Kidney 6 (*Zhaohai*)
4. Liver 3 (*Taichong*)
5. Large Intestine 4 (*Hoku*)
6. Bladder 18 (*Gan Shu*)

See the Appendix, pp. 131–38 for the description and location of points.

Herbal Remedies

Take a combination of Hsiao Yao Wan (Relaxed Wanderer) with horsetail, ginkgo biloba, milk thistle and dandelion — available from Integral Health Apothecary and Starfire International (see Resources). Take 8 pills 3 times a day, or 12 pills twice a day. In tincture form, follow the instructions on the bottle. Take 1 teaspoon of the mixture of other herbs twice a day.

Homeopathic   Consult a trained homeopath who can recommend the
Remedies   appropriate constitutional remedy for you with regard to
                  your floaters.

Exercises   Do 20 minutes of both aerobic and eye exercises at least
                  four times per week (see Chapter 1).

Spinal   Consult a qualified chiropractor or osteopath to make
Manipulation   sure that the spine and neck are free from any energy
                  blocks that might cause poor circulation and, thus, lack
                  of energy to the eyes.

Eye   Wear a hat and good ultraviolet filtering glasses when
Protection   outdoors.

CHAPTER 8

Conjunctivitis or "Pink Eye"

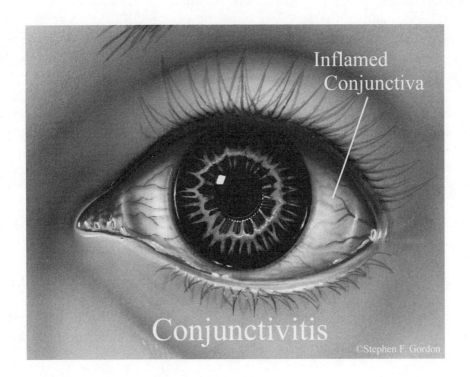

Inflamed Conjunctiva

Conjunctivitis

©Stephen F. Gordon

Every parent — and every teacher and day care worker, for that matter — can recognize conjunctivitis or "pink eye," the inflammation of the *conjunctiva,* or mucous membrane that lines the inner eyelid and the eyeball. Usually caused by bacteria, conjunctivitis can sweep through a classroom or day care center in a few hours. Fortunately, there are simple and safe remedies for this scourge of the playground. But, first, just in case you don't know it when you see it, let's talk about the symptoms.

Conjunctivitis is the most common eye disease in the Western hemisphere. Because of its exposed position, the conjunctiva comes into contact with more microorganisms than any other membrane. Most cases are caused by bacteria, such as pneumococcus, staphylococcus or streptococcus, although allergies and some viruses can also cause conjunctivitis.

How do you know if you (or your child) have conjunctivitis? There is usually an acute onset of redness, swelling, lots of tearing, a yellow discharge, and, although there usually is no pain, sometimes there is an itchy, there's-something-in-my-eye feeling. And if it occurs overnight, which frequently occurs because closed eyelids create a nice warm atmosphere for the invading bacteria to grow, the eyelids will probably be stuck together upon awakening in the morning. This is usually the diagnostic indicator of conjunctivitis.

The infection usually starts in one eye and is spread to the other quite readily. Like colds and the flu, conjunctivitis is spread quite easily from one person to another through commonly used items, such as towels, toys, doorknobs, handshakes, etc. And, also like colds and flu, it pays to keep the hands, fingernails and nasal passages clean.

PREVENTION AND TREATMENT

Conventional medicine usually prescribes sulfa-based eyedrops once other potential problems have been ruled out. These usually work within three days; if they don't, broad-spectrum antibiotics are prescribed. But we have found that nutrition, acupressure, herbs and homeopathic remedies are successful ways of treating conjunctivitis without drugs.

The Vision Diet

In addition to the basic Vision Diet outlined in Chapter 1, eating yogurt, as well as applying it in a compress to the eyes, will help alleviate conjunctivitis. The acidophilus in yogurt combats the bacterial infection. For that reason, we also suggest acidophilus supplements. Eat ½ cup of yogurt with live cultures three times a day or take an acidophilus supplement (with about six billion live or probiotic organisms) three times a day.

Vitamins and Minerals

The following are some of the essential nutrients for treating conjunctivitis. Other recommended nutrients can be found in the Conjunctivitis Treatment Program at the end of this chapter.

Vitamin A. We've discussed vitamin A's role in eye health in other chapters, but it is especially important in promoting the health of all epithelial tissues, including the conjunctiva.

Vitamin B complex. Conjunctivitis can be triggered by a vitamin B2 deficiency, but supplementing with the entire B complex can increase the availability of vitamin B2 without inducing deficiencies of the other B vitamins.

Traditional Chinese Medicine

In Traditional Chinese Medicine, conjunctivitis indicates imbalances and/or deficiencies in the lung and spleen meridians. The strategy in the treatment of conjunctivitis is to choose herbs and acupressure points to build the lung qi, which helps protect the eyes from invasion from environmental pathogens such as bacteria and viruses. We also focus on removing dampness from the spleen meridian, which manifests in irritated eyelids and sticky secretions in the eyes.

Acupressure

See the Conjunctivitis Prevention Program at the end of this chapter for the acupressure points that have long been used in the treatment of conjunctivitis.

Herbal Remedies

In the treatment of conjunctivitis, we recommend a combination of Chinese and Western herbs. These herbs should be taken internally and applied externally as a compress to the infected eye.

The Chinese formula is called *Ming Mu Di Huang Wan* (Brighten the Eyes) and it is composed of rehmannia root, cornus fruit, dioscorea root, alisma root, poria fungus, moutan, lycii berries, chrysanthemum flower, red peony, tribulus fruit and haliotis shell. This is a classic tonic for visual problems that involve dry and/or hot situations, such as itchy or red eyes and conjunctivitis. It helps to nourish the kidneys, thus bringing more water and fluids to the eyes, in order to relieve a "hot" condition.

In addition to Ming Mu, take the following herbs, which fight infection, boost the immune system and nourish the eyes. Any of these herbs could also be made into a hot compress. Or, simply put herbal tea bags of any of these herbs which have been briefly immersed in warm water over your eyes.

Chamomile (Matricaria chamomilla) tea can be used as an eye wash to reduce the inflammation of conjunctivitis. Place two chamomile tea bags in one cup of boiling water; let steep 10 minutes, cool slightly, and use as an eye wash.

Cleavers (Galium aparine) is a good tonic and one of the best for supporting the lymphatic system. It helps the body detoxify, is a natural diuretic and boosts the body's self-healing abilities.

Echinacea (Echinacea angustifolia) is a popular immune system booster and also has antibacterial and antiseptic capabilities.

Eyebright (Euphrasia officinalis) has been used to treat eye ailments since the Middle Ages. It is especially good for eye inflammations and redness.

Goldenseal (Hydrastis canadensis) is valued for its antiseptic and antibiotic properties. It reduces infection and inflammation and has been used for more than 100 years by American herbalists to heal eye inflammations.

Honeysuckle (Lonicerae japonicae) has been shown to inhibit viral and bacterial infections, such as those from staphylococcus, streptococcus and salmonella, the bacteria that can cause conjunctivitis.

Red raspberry leaf (Rubus idaeus), an astringent, helps loosen mucous discharge from the eyes.

Calendula (Calendula officinalis) is a very effective herb in the treatment of inflammatory conditions when used externally.

A good remedy would combine the Chinese remedy, Ming Mu with the herbs listed above. Make a compress using this mixture or any of the individual herbs and apply it two to three times a day.

Homeopathic Remedies[1]

There are several homeopathic remedies helpful in the treatment of conjunctivitis.

Belladonna is used in the early stages of conjunctivitis when the eyes suddenly appear bright red, hot and throbbing. Tears will flow and there will be sensitivity to light.

Euphrasia is indicated when the eyes and lids are red and the discharge may be thick with mucus. The eyes will feel dry and sandy.

Apis is used when the conjunctiva becomes swollen. The eyes will be red with a lot of hot tears and the eyelids may be puffy as well. Cold compresses are also helpful along with this remedy.

Pulsatilla is called for when the redness is accompanied by a thick yellow/greenish discharge. The eyes may itch and burn, especially towards evening. The lid margins may be extremely itchy. If exposure to fresh air and bathing the eyes in cold water are helpful, this is the remedy to try.

Hepar sulph is a good choice if there is a thick pus-like discharge or if warmth makes the eyes feel better (and coldness makes them feel worse).

If symptoms persist over one week, see your physician or consult a qualified homeopath.

Other Remedies

Similisan eye drops #1 (or #2 for allergic irritation) or eye drops of colloidal silver also are beneficial for a speedy recovery.

CASE STUDY

A woman visiting from Japan had developed acute conjunctivitis after swimming in contaminated water. She sought natural remedies rather than drugs. Our first recommendations were to discontinue wearing her contact lenses and, of course, to avoid swimming in the contaminated water.

We recommended the Conjunctivitis Prevention Program. After three days of following many of the recommendations in the program, her eyes looked normal. She waited one more week to be sure all toxins were eliminated from her system before she began to wear her contact lenses again.

Conjunctivitis Prevention Program

Vision Diet	*Follow the Vision Diet in Chapter 1 as closely as possible.*

- Plain yogurt is especially beneficial.
- Avoid all sugars.
- Drink 8–10 glasses of water per day, but not with meals — 30 minutes before a meal or 2 hours after a meal.

Nutritional Supplements	*Take the following vitamins and minerals on a daily basis:*

Vitamin A	5,000–10,000 I.U.
Beta-carotene	10,000–25,000 I.U.
Vitamin B1 (thiamin)	100 mg
B2 (riboflavin)	100 mg
B3 (niacin)	100 mg
B5 (pantothenic acid)	500 mg
B6 (pyroxidine)	100 mg
Folic acid	1,000 mcg
B12 (cobalamin)	100 mcg
Choline	100 mg
Inositol	100 mg
Biotin	500 mcg
Vitamin C	1,500 mg (buffered form)
Vitamin D	200 I.U.
Vitamin E	400–800 I.U.
Zinc	30 mg
Chromium	200 mcg
Selenium	200 mcg
Calcium	500 mg for men, 800 mg for women
Magnesium	500 mg
Quercetin	2,000 mg
Rutin	300 mg
Omega-3 oils	1,500 mg
Omega-6 oils	1,500 mg

Acupressure Points	Massage each point for 30 seconds, twice a day:

Acupressure Points   *Massage each point for 30 seconds, twice a day:*

1. Bladder 1 (*Jing Ming*)
2. Gall Bladder 1 (*Tonziliao*)
3. Large Intestine 4 (*Hegu*)
4. Liver 2 (*Xingjian*)
5. Stomach 44 (*Neiting*)
6. Triple Burner 23 (*Sizhukong*)
7. Bladder 10 (*Tian Zhu*)

See the Appendix, pp. 131–38 for the description and location of points.

Herbal Remedies   Take a combination of Ming Mu Di Huang Wan (Brighten the Eyes) with chamomile, cleavers, echinacea, eyebright, goldenseal, honeysuckle, red raspberry leaf and calendula — available from Integral Health Apothecary and Starfire International (see Resources). Take 12 pills 3 times a day, and 1 teaspoon of the mixture of other herbs twice a day.

Homeopathic Remedies   Consult a trained homeopath who can recommend the appropriate constitutional remedy for you with regard to your conjunctivitis, or try Belladonna, Euphrasia, Apis, Pulsatilla or Hepar Sulph.

Other Remedies   Similisan eye drops #1 (or #2 for allergic irritation) or eye drops of colloidal silver.

Exercises   Do 20 minutes of both aerobic and eye exercises at least four times per week (see Chapter 1).

Spinal Manipulation   Consult a qualified chiropractor or osteopath to make sure that the spine and neck are free from any energy blocks that might cause poor circulation and, thus, lack of energy to the eyes.

Appendix

ACUPRESSURE DIRECTIONS[1]

Applying pressure. Use the ball of your thumb and apply firm pressure to the point you have chosen. Hold steady pressure for one to two minutes on each point. Each point will feel different when you apply pressure to it; some will feel sore or achy, some tense, some will have no feeling at all.

The amount of pressure should be firm enough to feel the pressure, but not too hard to create a painful experience.

Environment. Try to wear comfortable clothing when doing your acupressure session and keep your fingernails short. Find a quiet environment in which you will not be distracted during this healing activity.

Time. Do not do acupressure right before or right after a meal. Try to do acupressure treatments a minimum of four times per week.

Breathing. Remember to breathe. Breathing is the most powerful and effective way to purify and revitalize the body. Deep breathing helps the cells of your eyes receive the oxygen they need for healing. Practice long, slow, concentrated abdominal breathing while applying acupressure.

Cautions. If you are pregnant, consult a trained acupuncturist before treating yourself. Do not work on an area if it has a scar, burn or infection.

ACUPUNCTURE POINTS

Bladder 1 (BL1) — Jing Ming — Eye Brightness
Brings energy to the eyes. It is a powerful intersecting point for many meridians.
Location: In the inner corner of each eye, just above the tear duct.

Bladder 2 (BL2) — Zan Zhu — Collection of Bamboo
Brings energy to the eyes.
Location: At the nose side of each eyebrow.

Bladder 10 (BL 10) — Tian Zhu — Heaven's Pillar
Brings energy to the eyes.
Location: A half inch below the base of the skull in the back of the neck, level
    with the space between the first and second cervical vertebrae approximately
    three quarters of an inch out from either side of the spine.

Bladder 18 (BL 18) — Gan Shu — Liver's Hollow
Helps with blood flow to the eyes, especially for liver-related eye syndromes such
    as glaucoma.
Location: Approximately 1.5 inches away from either side of the spine at the
    level of the lower end of the ninth thoracic vertebrae.

Bladder 23 (BL 23) — Shen Shu — Kidney's Hollow
Brings energy to the eyes, especially for kidney-related eye syndromes such as
    cataracts and dry eyes.
Location: In the lower back (between the second and third lumbar vertebrae) ap-
    proximately 1.5 inches away from either side of the spine at waist level.

Bladder 62 (BL62) — Shen Mai — Extending Vessel
Helps with the drainage of eye fluids as in, for example, glaucoma.
Location: In the depression directly below the outside ankle bone.

Gall Bladder 1 (GB1) — Tong Zi Liao — Pupil's Seam
Brings energy to the eyes.
Location: At the lateral end of each eye.

Gall Bladder 14 (GB14) — Yangbai — Yang Brightness
Helps clear and brighten the eyes.
Location: Directly above the pupil, approximately one inch above the eyebrow.

Gall Bladder 20 (GB20) — Feng Chi — Wind Pool
Brings energy (brightness) to the eyes. It is used for all eye disorders. This point
     commands the cervical sympathetic nervous system.
Location: In the hollow below the occipital bone at the back of the head.

Gall Bladder 37 (GB37) — Guang Ming — Bright Light
Brightens and "opens" the eyes.
Location: Approximately five inches above the outside ankle bone on the ante-
     rior border of the fibula.

Governor Vessel 23 (GV23) — Shang Xing — Upper Star
Brings energy (brightness) to the eyes. It is good for glaucoma, cataracts and
     corneal inflammations.
Location: Approximately one inch within the interior hairline on the midline of
     the head.

Kidney 3 (KI3) — Taixi — Great Creek
A major energy point for the kidneys.
Location: At the midpoint between the inside ankle bone and the Achilles ten-
     don.

Kidney 6 (KI6) — Zhaohai — Shining Sea
The best point on the kidney meridian to nourish yin deficiency. It helps nourish
     fluids and moisten dryness of the eyes.
Location: One thumb width below the inside of the ankle bone.

Large Intestine 4 (LI4) — Hoku — Union of the Valleys
Helps brighten the eyes, helps with colon congestion and disperses stuck energy
     in the head and neck areas. Do not use if pregnant.
Location: In the webbing between the thumb and index finger, at the highest spot
     of the muscle that protrudes when the thumb and index finger are brought
     close together.

Liver 2 (LV2) — Xingjian — Walk Between
Takes heat away from the eyes; good for conjunctivitis.
Location: In the web between the first and second toe.

Liver 3 (LV3) — Tai Chang — Great Rushing
The main point for the liver meridian. Liver 3 is used when the liver energy is constrained or deficient. In Chinese medicine, the liver is thought to open into the eyes; therefore, the Chinese believe that the liver rules internal and external problems with vision. This point helps bring energy to brighten the eyes and helps resolve physiological and psychological problems with vision.
Location: On the upper aspect of the foot, in the depression between the big toe and the second toe.

Liver 8 (LV8) — Qu Quan — Spring and Bend
Helps supply blood to the liver meridian which nourishes the eyes.
Location: On the inside of the knee, where the crease ends when the knee is bent.

Pericardium 6 (PC6) — Nei Guan — Inner Border Gate
Helps regulate the liver, relaxes the mind and balances the emotions. It is good for conjunctivitis and other inflammations of the eyes.
Location: Approximately two inches above the crease in the middle of the wrist.

Qiuhou — Behind the Ball
In the obicularis oculi muscle.
Location: On the inferior border of the orbit, directly below the lateral (outer end) of the eye.

Spleen 6 (SP6) — Sanyinjiao — Three Yin Junction
Helps benefit the spleen, liver and kidney energies.
Location: Approximately four inches above the inside ankle bone.

Stomach 1 (ST1) — Chengqi — Contain Tears
On the lower eyelid, where tears are stored and released.
Location: Directly below the pupil on the orbital rim.

Stomach 36 (ST36) — Zu San Li — Walks Three Miles
Brings energy and blood to the eyes. It helps with the visual acuity of elderly patients.
Location: Three inches below the dimple or depression on the outside of the knee; approximately an inch from the crest of the shinbone, ST36 lies in a groove or natural depression in the muscle.

Stomach 44 (ST44) — Neiting — Inner Courtyard
Helps remove heat from the eyes, good for conjunctivitis and sties.
Location: In between where toes two and three meet the foot, on the lateral side of the second toe.

Tai Yang — Sun
Brings energy to the eyes.
Location: In the depression one inch below the end of the eyebrow and the outer end of the eye.

Triple Burner 23 (TB23) — Si Zhu Kong — Silken Bamboo Hole
This point influences the orbital hollow (shaped like bamboo) which houses the eyes. It brings energy to the eyes.
Location: In the depression at the lateral end of the eyebrow.

Ying Tang — Seal Hall
Calms the mind and brings energy to the eyes.
Location: At the midpoint between the two eyebrows.

Yu Yao — Fish Waist
Brings energy to the eyes.
Location: In the hollow at the middle of the eyebrow above the pupil of the eye.

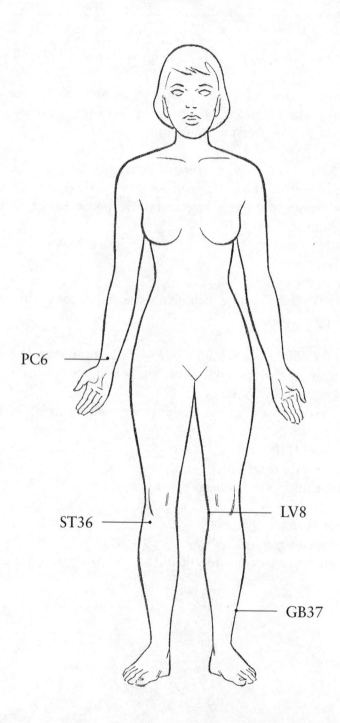

PC6

ST36

LV8

GB37

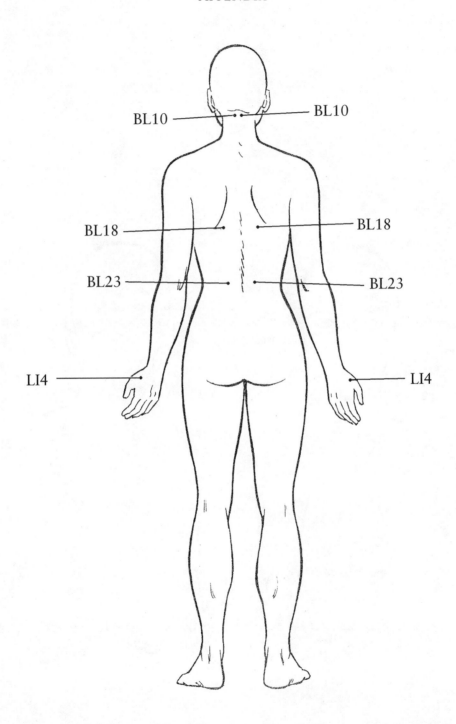

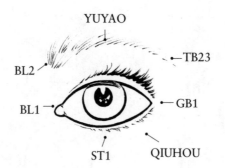

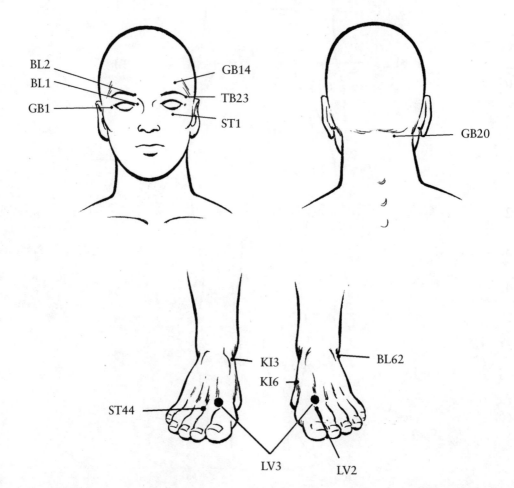

References

Due to the enormous amount of research that went into this book, rather than fill it with endless footnotes, the following are the references most directly related to the information in each chapter.

CHAPTER 1

1. Sussman, M. *Program for Better Vision*. MA: Cambridge Institute for Better Vision, 1985.
2. Sutton, A. *Vision, Intelligence, and Creativity 1.9*. Optometric Extension Program, Santa Ana, CA, p. 58–59.
3. Chang, T.S. *The Complete Book of Acupuncture*. Berkeley, CA: Celestial Arts, 1976.
4. Elias, J., and Masline, R.S. *Healing Herbal Remedies*. NY: Dell Publishing, 1995.

Other references used in this chapter

Advanced Medical Nutrition, Inc. Catalog. Hayward, CA, (800) 437-8888.
Gach, R.M. *Acupressure Potent Points*. NY: Bantam, 1990.
Veith, I., trans. *The Yellow Emperor's Classic of Internal Medicine*, Berkeley, CA: Univ. of CA Press, 1949.

CHAPTER 2

1. Lee, P. Economic concerns in glaucoma management in the 21st century. *Journal of Glaucoma* 2 (1993): 148–50.
2. Stocker, F.W. New ways of influencing the intraocular pressure. *New York State Medical Journal* 49 (1949): 58–63.
3. Stocker, F.W., Holt, L.B., and Clower, J.W. Clinical experiments with new ways of influencing intraocular tension. *Archives of Ophthalmology* 40 (1948): 46–55.
4. Berens, C. et al. Allergy in glaucoma: Manifestations of allergy in three glaucoma patients as determined by the pulse-diet method of coca. *Annals of Allergy* 5 (1947): 526–35.
5. Sakai, T., Murata, M., and Amemiya, T. Effect of long-term treatment of glaucoma with vitamin B12. *Glaucoma* 14 (1992): 167–70.
6. Albrick, P.H., Angle closure surveys in Greenland Eskimos, *Canadian Journal of Ophthalmology* 8 (1973): 260–64.
7. Mancio, M., Ohia, E., and Kulkarni, P. A comparative study between cod liver oil and liquid lard intake on intraocular pressure on rabbits. *Prostaglandins Leukotrienes and Essential Fatty Acids* 45 (1992): 239–43.
8. Samples, J.R., Krause, G., and Lewy, A.J. Effect of melatonin on intraocular pressure. *Current Eye Research* 7 (1988): 649–78.
9. Passo, M.S. et al. Regular exercise lowers intraocular pressure in glaucoma patients. *Investigative Ophthalmology* 35. In ARVO Abstracts, March 15, 1994.
10. Martin, B.J. et al. Ocular hypotension after exercise. *Investigative Ophthalmology* 35 (1994): 191–95.
11. Ripley, H.S., and Wolff, H.G. Life situation, emotions and glaucoma. *Psychosomatic Medicine* 12 (1948): 215–24.
12. Grignolo, F.M. et al. Variations of intraocular pressure induced by psychological stress. *Klinische Monatsblaten Augenheilkd* 170 (1977): 562–69.
13. Stocker, F.W., Holt, L.B., and Clower, J.W. Clinical experiments with new ways of influencing intraocular tension. *Archives of Ophthalmology* 40 (1948): 46–55.
14. Croll, M.C., and Croll, L.J. Emotional glaucoma. *American Journal of Ophthalmology* 49 (1960): 297–305.

15. Cooler, P., and Gregg, J.M. Effect of delta-9-tetrahydrocannabinol on intraocular pressure in humans. *S outhern Medical Journal* 70 (1977): 951–54.
16. Langan, L.M., and Watkins, S.M. Pressure of menswear on the neck in relation to visual performance. *Human Factors* 29 (1987): 67–71.

Other references used in this chapter

Adams, B.A., and Brubaker, R.F. Caffeine has no clinically significant effect on aqueous humor flow in the normal human eye. *Ophthalmology* 97 (1990): 1030–31.

Asregadoo, E.R. Blood levels of thiamine and ascorbic acid in chronic open-angle glaucoma. *Annals of Ophthalmology* 11 (1979): 1095–1100.

Balch, J.F., and Balch, P.A. *Prescription for Nutritional Healing*. Garden City Park, NY: Avery Publishing Group, 1990.

Baxter, R.C. Vitamin C and Glaucoma. *Journal of the American Optometric Association* 59 (June 1988): 438.

Buckingham, T., and Young, R. The rise and fall of intraocular pressure: The influence of physiological factors. *Ophthalmology Physiological Optics* 6 (1986): 95–99.

Caprioli, J., and Sears, M. Forskolin lowers intraocular pressure in rabbits, monkeys, and man. *Lancet* I (1983): 958–60.

Caputo, B.J., and Katz, L.J. The quality of life of the glaucoma patient in the light of treatment modalities. *Current Opinion in Ophthalmology* 5.2 (1994): 10–14.

Cohen, S.I., and Hajoff, J. Life events and the onset of acute closed-angle glaucoma. *Journal of Psychosomatic Research* 16 (1972): 355–61.

Duke-Elder, W.S. *Textbook of Ophthalmology*, Vol. 1. St. Louis: C.B. Mosby Co., 1948.

Feldman, R.M., Steinmann, W.C., Spaeth, G.L., and Varma, R. Effects of altered daily fluid intake on intraocular pressure in glaucoma patients. *Glaucoma* 9 (1987): 118–21.

Gaspar, A.Z., Gasser, P., and Glammer, J. The influence of magnesium on visual field and peripheral vasospasm in glaucoma. *Ophthalmologica* 209 (1995): 11–13.

Guzman, G. et al. Glaucoma in the United States population: The economic burden of illness. *Investigative Ophthalmology* 331 (1992). In ARVO Abstracts 327.

Inada, K. et al. Increase of aqueous humor proteins with aging. *Japanese Journal of Ophthalmology* 32 (1988): 126–31.

Kiuchi, Y. et al. Exercise intensity determines the magnitude of iop decrease after running. *Japanese Journal of Ophthalmology* 38 (1994): 191–95.

Kreutner, W., Chapman, R.W. et al. Bronchodilation and antiallergy activity of forskolin. *European Journal of Pharmacology* 111 (1985): 1–8.

Krishna, S.M., and Shukla, P.K. Vitamin A and primary glaucoma. *Glaucoma* 4 (1982): 226–27.

Lane, B.C. Elevation of intraocular pressure with daily, sustained closework stimulus to accommodation to lowered tissue chromium and dietary deficiency of ascorbic acid (vitamin C). Ph.D. diss., New York Univ., 1980.

Lane, B.C. Interaction of diet, environment & activities on the glaucomas. Presented at College of Syntonic Optometry, May 6, 1995.

Leonard, T.J.K., Kerr-Muir, M.G., and Kirkby, G.R. Ocular hypertension and posture. *British Journal of Ophthalmology* 67 (1983): 1673–76.

Leydhecker, W., and Krieglestein, G.K. *Glaucoma Update II.* Berlin: Springer-Verlag, 1983, p. 95–102.

Linner, E. Intraocular pressure regulation and ascorbic acid. *Acta Soc. Med. Upsal.* 69 (1964): 225–32.

Linner, E. The pressure lowering effects of ascorbic acid in ocular hypertension. *Acta Ophthalmologica* (Copenhagen) 47 (1969): 685–89.

Lucidi, E.A. Glaucoma: Nutrition and healthy living can help!*The Holistic Optometrist* 5 (1987): 2–3.

Martin, B.J. et al. Exercise training reduces intraocular pressure among subjects suspected of having glaucoma. *Archives of Ophthalmology* 109 (1991): 1096–98.

Mayhan, W.G., Rubestein, I. Acetycholine induces vasoconstricitoni of the microcirculation of cardiomyopathic hamsters: Reversal by L-arginine. *Biochemical and Biophysical Research Communications* 184 (1992): 1372–77.

Mehra, K.S., Roy, P.N., and Khare, B.B. Tobacco smoking and glaucoma. *Annals of Ophthalmology* 8 (1976): 462–64.

Meyer, B.H. et al. The effects of forskolin eye drops on intraocular pressure. South African Medical Journal 71.9 (1987): 570–71.

Moffat, J.L. *Homeopathic Therapeutics in Ophthalmology.* New Delhi: B. Jain Publishers, 1982, p. 132.

Moses, R.A., Preston, L., and Wette, R. Horizontal gaze postion effect on intraocular pressure. *Investigative Ophthalmology* 22 (1982): 551–53.

Norton, A.B. *Ophthalmic Diseases and Therapeutics.* New Delhi: B. Jain Publishers, reprinted 1987, p. 480.

Opatowsky, I. et al. Intraocular pressure elevation associated with inhalation and nasal corticosteroids. *Ophthalmology* 102 (1995): 177–79.

Passo, M.S. et al. Exercise training reduces intraocular pressure among subjects suspected of having glaucoma. *Archives of Ophthalmology* 109 (1991): 1096–98.

Pizzorno, J.E. and Murray, M.T. *A Textbook of Natural Medicine,* Vol. 1. Seattle: John Bastyr College Publications, 1987.

Ralston, N.C. Successful treatment and management of acute glaucoma using acupuncture. *American Journal of Acupuncture* 5 (1977): 283.

Raymond, L.F. Allergy and chronic simple glaucoma. *Annals of Allergy* 22 (1964): 146–50.

Rice, R., and Allen, R.C. Yoga in glaucoma. *American Journal of Ophthalmology* 69 (1970): 608–10.

Rotberg, M.H. Biofeedback for ophthalmologic disorders. *Survey of Ophthalmology* 27 (1983): 381–86.

Russell, P., Koretz, J., and Epstein, D.L. Is primary open angle glaucoma caused by small proteins?*Medical Hypotheses* 41 (1993): 455–58.

Sardi, B. Glaucoma: Anti-Glaucoma regimen emphasizing non-pharmacologic therapy and lifestyle changes, Part 3 of a 3-Part Series. *Townsend Letter for Doctors & Patients* (Jan. 1996): 63.

Sardi, B. Glaucoma: Underlying factor, Part 2. *Townsend Letter for Doctors & Patients* (Dec. 1995): 46–51.

Schoenberg, M.J. Role of state of anxiety in the pathogenesis of primary glaucoma. *Archives of Ophthalmology* 49 (1960): 297–305.

Seelig, M.S. Magnesium, antioxidants, and myocardial infarction. *Journal of American College of Nutrition* 13 (1994): 116–17.

Seto, C. et al. Acute effects of topical forskolin on aqueous humor dynamics in man. *Japanese Journal of Ophthalmology* 30 (1986): 238–44.

Shepard, R.J. et al. Effects of cigarette smoking on intraocular pressure and vision. *British Journal of Ophthalmology* 62 (1978): 682–87.

Sjogren, H. Allergically conditioned changes in the intraocular pressure. *Acta Ophthalmologica* 16 (1938): 542–47.

Stewart, W.C., Crinkley, C.M.C., and Murrell, H.P. Cigarette-smoking in normal subjects, ocular hypertensive, and chronic open-angle glaucoma patients. *American Journal of Ophthalmology* 117 (1994): 267–68.

Virno, M. et al. Oral treatment of glaucoma with vitamin C. *Eye, Ear, Nose, & Throat Monthly* 46 (1967): 1502–08.

Weinreb, R.N. Effect of inverted body position on intraocular pressure. *American Journal of Ophthalmology* 98 (1984): 784–87.

Wilson, R.M. et al. A case-control study of risk factors in open angle glaucoma. *Archives of Ophthalmology* 105 (1987): 1066–71.

CHAPTER 3

1. Christen, W.G. et al. Cigarette smoking and the risks of cataract. *Investigative Ophthalmology*. In ARVO Abstracts, April 1991.

2. Christen, W.G., and Seddon, J.M. Cigarette smoking and cataract. *American Journal of Preventive Medicine* 9 (1993): 65–66.

3. Lane, B.C. Fish methylmercury and human cataractogenesis. Presented at the American Academy of Optometry Meeting, December 13, 1992.

4. Gaby, A.R., and Wright, J.V. Nutritional Factors in Degenerative Eye Disorders: Cataract and Macular Degeneration. Wright/Gaby Nutrition Institute, 1991.

5. Blondin, J., Baragi, V.K., Schwartz, E.R., Sadowski, J., and Taylor, A. Prevention of eye lens protein damage by dietary vitamin C. *Federal Proceedings* 45 (1986): 478.

6. Bouton, S.M. Vitamin C and the aging eye. *Archives of Internal Medicine* 63 (1939): 930–45.

7. Bhat, K.S. Plasma calcium and trace metals in human subjects with mature cataract. *Nutrition Reports International* 37 (1988): 157–63.

8. Robertson, J.M. A possible role for vitamins C and E in cataract prevention. *American Journal of Clinical Nutrition* 53 (1991): 346S–351S.

9. Teikari, J. Prevention of cataract with alpha-tocopherol and beta carotene. *Investigative Ophthalmological Visual Science* 33 (1992): 1307.

10. Bravetti, G.O. Preventive medical treatment of senile cataract with vitamin E and Vaccinium myrtillus anthocyanosides: Clinical evaluation. *Ann Ottalmol Clinical Ocul.* 115 (1989): 109.

Other references used in this chapter

Abel, R. Can eating right preserve your sight? *Review of Optometry* (July 1993): 65–68.

Atkinson, D.T. Malnutrition as an etiological factor in senile cataract. *Eye, Ear, Nose and Throat Monthly* 31 (1952): 79–83.

Balch, J.F., and Balch, P.A. *Prescription for Nutritional Healing.* Garden City Park, NY: Avery Publishing Group, 1990.

Bellows, J. Biochemistry of the lens: Some studies on vitamin C and lens. *Archives of Ophthalmology* 16 (1936): 58.

Birouez-Aragon, I. et al. The effects of sugars on the lens. *Ophthalmologie* 7 (1993): 51–54.

Burnett, J.C. *Curability of Cataract with Medicines.* New Delhi: B. Jain Publishers, 1989.

Cataract as an outcome of zinc deficiency in salmon. *Nutrition Reviews* 44.3 (1986): 118–20.

Chandra, D.B., Varma, R., Ahmad S., and Varma, S.D. Vitamin C in the human aqueous humor and cataracts. *International Journal of Vitamin and Nutrition Research* 56 (1986): 165–68.

Clark, J.I. Cataract inhibitor slated for clinical trials. *Ophthalmology Times* (July 1, 1992): 13.

Couet, C. et al. Lactose and cataract in humans: A review. *Journal of the American College of Nutrition* 10.1 (1991): 79–86.

Cuthbert, J. et al. Diuretic drugs as risk factors in cataractogenesis. *Metabolic, Pediatric and Systemic Ophthalmology* 10 (1987): 48–54.

Duarte, A. *Cataract Breakthrough.* Huntington Beach, CA: International Institute of Natural Health and Science, 1982, p. 149.

Duke-Elder, W.S. The pathological action of light upon the eye. *Lancet* (June 19, 1926): 1188–1254.

Fackelmann, K.A. Studies smoke out the risks of cataracts. *Science News* 142 (1992): 134.

Ferrer, J.V. et al. Senile cataract: A review on free radical related pathogenesis and antioxidant prevention. *Archives Gerontology* 13 (1991): 51–59.

Fujuhara, K. Treatment of cataracts of ba-wei-wan. *Journal of the Society of Oriental Medicine of Japan* 24 (1974): 465–79.

Hankinson, S.H. et al. Nutrient intake and cataract extraction in women: A prospective study. *British Medical Journal* 305 (August 8, 1992): 335–39.

Haranaka, R. et al. Pharmacological action of hachimijiogan (ba-wei-wan) on the metabolism of aged subjects. *American Journal of Chinese Medicine* 24 (1986): 59–67.

Heffley, J.D., and Williams, R.J. The nutritional teamwork approach: Prevention and regression of cataracts. *Proceedings of the National Academy of Science* 71 (1974): 4161–68.

Jacques, P.F. et al. Epidemiological evidence of a role for antioxidant vitamins and carotenoids in cataract prevention. *American Journal of Clinical Nutrition* 53 (1990): 352S–355S.

Jacques, P.F. et al. Nutritional status in persons with and without senile cataract: Blood vitamin and mineral levels. *American Journal of Clinical Nutrition* 48 (1988): 152–58.

Jacques, P.F., Chylack, L.T. Jr., McGandy, R.B., and Hartz, S.C. Antioxidant status in persons with and without senile cataract. *Archives of Ophthalmology* 106 (1988): 337–40.

Kamei, A. et al. The evaluation of therapeutic efficacy of hachimi-jio-gan (Traditional Chinese Medicine) to mouse hereditary cataract. *Journal of Ocular Pharmacology* 4.4 (1988): 311–19.

Lockie, A. *The Family Guide to Homeopathy.* New York: Simon & Schuster, 1989, p. 158.

Long, R.Y. Cataracts may respond to nutrients. *Health News & Review* (March/April 1989): 6.

Mitchell, H.S., and Dodge, W.M. Cataract in rats fed on high lactose rations. *Journal of Nutrition* 9 (1935): 37–49.

Moffat, J.L. *Homeopathic Therapeutics in Ophthalmology.* New Delhi, India: B. Jain Publishers, 1982, p. 132.

The Ocular Hazards of UV Exposure. Monograph, American Academy of Ophthalmology, Public Health Committee, June 25, 1989.

Pizzorno, J.E., and Murray, M.T. A *Textbook of Natural Medicine.* Vol. 1. Seattle: John Bastyr College Publications, 1987.

Rathbun, W.B., and Holleschau, A.M. The effects of age on glutathione synthesis enzymes in lenses of old world simians and prosimians. *Current Eye Research 11* (1992): 601–07.

Rathbun, W., and Hanson, S. Glutathione metabolic pathway as a scavenging system in the lens. *Ophthalmological Research 11* (1979): 172–76.

Robertson, J. Cataract prevention: Time for a clinical trial? *British Journal of Clinical Practice* 44.11 (1990): 475–76.

Rosner, L., Farmer, C.J., and Bellows, J. Biochemistry of the lens. Archives of Ophthalmology 20 (1938): 417–26.

Seddon et al. Vitamin supplementation and the risk of cataract. *Investigative Ophthalmology and Visual Science 33* (1992): 1097.

Skalka, H., and Prchal, J. Cataracts and riboflavin deficiency. *American Journal of Clinical Nutrition 34* (1981): 861–63.

Skalka, H.W. et al. Riboflavin deficiency and cataract formation. *Metabolic & Pediatric Ophthalmology* 5.1 (1981): 17–20.

Swanson, A., and Truesdale, A. Elemental analysis in normal and cataractous human lens tissue. *Biochemical and Biophysical Research Communications* 45 (1971): 1488–96.

Taylor, A. Associations between nutrition and cataract. *Nutrition Reviews* 47 (1989): 225–34.

Tupper, B., Miller, D., and Miller, R. The effect of a 550 nm cutoff filter on the vision of cataract patients. *Annals of Ophthalmology* 70 (1985): 38.

Van Kuijk, F. Effects of ultraviolet light on the eye: Role of protective glasses. *Environmental Health Perspectives* 96 (1991): 177–84.

Varma, S.D. et al. Scientific basis for medical therapy of cataracts by antioxidants. *American Journal of Clinical Nutrition* 53 (1991): 335S–345S.

Whanger, P., and Weswig, P. Effects of selenium, chromium and antioxidants on growth, eye cataracts, plasma cholesterol and blood glucose in selenium deficient, vitamin E supplemented rats. *Nutrition Reports International* 12 (1975): 345–58.

Young, R.W. *Age Related Cataract.* New York: Oxford Univ. Press, 1991.

Zigman, S. et al. Sunlight and human cataract: An epidemiologic investigation, *American Journal of Epidemiology* 105 (1997): 450–59.

CHAPTER 4

1. Sardi, B. *Nutrition and the Eyes*, Vol. 2. Health Spectrum Publishers, 1994, p. 13.
2. Liu, I.Y., White, L., and LaCroiz, A.Z. The association of age-related macular degeneration and lens opacitites in the aged. *American Journal of Public Health* 79 (1989): 765–69.
3. Vinding, R., Appleyard, M., Nyboe, J., and Jensen, G. Risk factor analysis for atarophic and exudative age-related macular degeneration. *Acta Ophythalmologica* 70 (1992): 66–72.
4. Lotti, K., and Grunwald, J.E. The effect of caffeine on the human macular circulation. *Investigative Ophthalmology* 32 (1991): 3028–32.
5. Munoz, B. et al. Blue light and risk of age-related macular degeneration. *Investigative Ophthalmology* 31. In ARVO Abstracts, March 15, 1990.
6. Koyanagi, T., Sone, K., Sugihara, S., and Tamura, A. Effect of riboflavin deficiency on rat electroretinogram. *Journal of Vitaminology* 12 (1966): 281–85.
7. Sternberg, P. Treating Age-Related Macular Degeneration. Presented at Science Writers Seminar in Ophthalmology: Research to Prevent Blindness, 1988.
8. Goldberg, J. et al. Factors associated with age-related macular degeneration: An analysis of data from the First National Health and Nutrition Examination Survey. *American Journal of Epidemiology* 128 (1988): 700–20.
9. Lane, B.C. Ascorbic acid, copper, zinc, superoxide dismutase, protein, transaminases, lipid peroxides, & sunlight exposure as risk factors for age-related macular degeneration. *Investigative Ophthalmology and Visual Science* 32.4: 1050. In ARVO Abstracts 1876.
10. Anderson, R.E., Rapp, L.M., and Wiegand, R.D. Lipid peroxidation and retinal degeneration. *Current Eye Research* 3 (1984): 223–27.
11. Connor, W.E., Neuringer, M., and Reisbick, S. Essential fatty acids: The importance of n-3 fatty acids in the retina and the brain. *Nutrition Reviews* 50 (1992): 21–29.
12. Stinson, A.M., Wiegand, R.D., and Anderson, R.E. Recycling of docosohexaenoic acid in rat retinas during n-3 fatty acid deficiency. *Journal of Lipid Research* 32 (1991): 2009–17.

13. O'Connor, D., and Pickles, V. New advances in macular degeneration. *Optometry Today* (April 1998): 22–26.

14. Wallace, L. The treatment of macular degeneration and other retinal diseases treated with light therapy, electrical stimulation, and nutrition using bioelectric therapy. *Journal of Optometric Phototherapy*, March 1997. For further information, call Dr. Larry Wallace in Ithaca, NY, at (607) 277–4749.

Other references used in this chapter

Adayeva, Y., Laychter, B.G., Lyev, P.A., Nayman, V.N., and Poletayeva, G.P. Vitamin E treatment in dystrophy of the macula lutea. *American Journal of Ophthalmology* 56 (1963): 498.

Age decreases the n-3 polyunsaturated fatty acids of the retina. *Nutrition Reviews* 47 (1989): 87–89.

Cruickshanks, K.J., and Klein, B.E.K. Sunlight and age-related macular degeneration. *Archives of Ophthalmology* 111 (1993): 514–18.

Drews, C.D. et al. Dietary antioxidants and age-related macular degeneration. *Investigative Ophthalmology* 34. In ARVO Abstracts 2237.

Eye Disease Case Control Study Group. Antioxidant status and neovascular age-related macular degeneration. *Archives of Ophthalmology* 111 (1993): 104–09.

Gaby, A.R., and Wright, J.V. Nutrititional Factors in Degenerative Eye Disorders: Cataract and Macular Degeneration. Wright/Gaby Nutrition Institute, 1991.

Gawande, A., and Marmor, M.F. The Specificity of Colored Lenses in Aiding Visual Performance in Retinal Disease. Report, Stanford Univ. Medical Center, 1991.

Hayes, K.C., Carey, R.E., and Shmidt, S.Y. Retinal degeneration associated with taurine deficiency in the cat. *Science* 188 (1975): 949–51.

Hyman, L. et al. Risk factors for age-related maculopathy. *Investigative Ophthalmology* 33. In ARVO Abstracts 548.

Kana, J.S. Effect of long-term aspirin therapy on ophthalmic artery blood flow in patients with carotid atherosclerotic disease. *Investigative Ophthalmology* 34. In ARVO Abstracts 3410.

Lane, B.C. *Nutrition and Vision.* New Canaan, CT: Keats Publishing, Inc., 1996.

Lebuisson, D.A., Leroy, L., and Rigal, G. Treatment of senile macular degeneration with Ginkgo biloba extract: A preliminary double-blind, drug versus placebo study. *Presse Med* 15 (1986): 1556–58.

Mares-Perlman, J.A. et al. Relationships between age-related maculopathy and intake of vitamin and mineral supplements. *Investigative Ophthalmology* 34. In ARVO Abstracts 2121.

Newsome, D.A., Swatz, M., Leone, N.C., Elston, R.C., and Miller, E. Oral zinc in macular degeneration. *Archives of Ophthalmology* 106 (1988): 192–198.

Paetkau, M.E. et al. Sinele disciform macular degeneration and smoking. *Canadian Journal of Ophthalmology* 13 (1978): 67–71.

Pincemail, J., and Deby, C. Anti-radical properties of Ginkgo biloba extract. *Presse Med* 15(1986): 1475–79.

Pizzorno, J., and Murray, M. *Encyclopedia of Natural Medicine.* Rocklin, CA: Prima, 1990.

Somerville-Large, L.B. A note on the clinical value of rutin in ophthalmology. *Transactions of the Ophthalmological Society United Kingdom* 69 (1950): 615–17.

Werbach, M., and Murray, M.T. *Botanical Influences on Illness. A Sourcebook of Clinical Research.* Tarzana, CA: Third Line Press, 1994, p. 310.

West, S., Vitale, S., Hallfrisch, J. et al. Are antioxidants or supplements protective for age-related macular degeneration? *Archives of Ophthalmology* 112.2 (1994): 222–27.

West, S.K. et al. Exposure to sunlight and other risk factors for age-related macular degeneration. *Archives of Ophthalmology* 107 (1989): 875–79.

Wright, J.V., Ogle, D.J., and Hoare, L. Improvement of vision in macular degeneration associated with intravenous zinc and selenium therapy: Two cases. *Journal of Nutrition and Medicine* 1 (1990): 133–38.

Young, R.W. Pathophysiology of age-related macular degeneration. *Survey of Ophthalmology* 31 (1987): 291–306.

Young, R.W. Solar radiation and age-related macular degeneration. *Survey of Ophthalmology* 32 (1988): 252–69.

CHAPTER 5

1. Memmert, R. Americans fall short of eyecare goals. *20/20* (September 1990): 44.
2. Laflamme, M.Y., and Swieca, R. A comparative study of two preservative-free tear substitutes in the management of severe dry eye. *Canadian Journal of Ophthalmology* 23 (1988): 174–76.
3. Winfield, A.J., Jessiman, D., Williams, A., and Esakowitz, L. A study of the causes on non-compliance by patients prescribed eyedrops. *British Journal of Ophthalmology* 74 (1990): 238–42.
4. White, W.L. Eye drops work better with two minutes of shuteye. *American Academy of Ophthalmology News Release*, October 28, 1990.
5. Zimmerman, T.J. Getting a drop on the eye. *Research to Prevent Blindness Science Writers Seminar*.
6. Tuberville, A. et al. Punctal occlusion in tear deficiency syndrome. *Ophthalmology* 89 (1982): 1170–72.
7. Manthorpe, R. et al. Primary Sjogren's syndrome treated with Efamol. *Danish Rheumatology Society* (June 1983).
8. Horrobin, D.F. *Clinical Uses of Essential Fatty Acids*, Eden Press, 1982, p. 129–37.

Other references used in this chapter

Barton-Goldberg Group, ed. *Alternative Medicine*. Fife, WA: Future Medicine Publishers, Inc., 1994, p. 936–37.

Basu, P.K. et al.The effect of cigarette smoke on the human tear film. *Canadian Journal of Ophthalmology* 13 (1978): 22–26.

Bergmann, M.T., Newman, B.L., and Johnson, N.C., Jr. The effect of a diuretic (hydrochlorthiazide) on tear production in humans. *American Journal of Ophthalmology* 99.4 (1985): 473–75.

Boyle, J. The digestive system and Sjogrens syndrome. *Sjogrens Digest* 4 (1993): 5.

Burns, E., and Mulley, G.P. Practical problems with eye drops among elderly ophthalmology outpatients. *Age and Ageing* 21 (1992): 168–70.

Fraunfelder, F.T., and Meyer, S.M. *Drug Induced Ocular Side Effects and Drug Interactions*, 2nd ed. Philadelphia: Lea & Febiger, 1982.

Gobbels, M., and Lemp, M. Artificial tears: Preservative's role evaluated. *Ophthalmology Times* (February 15, 1992): 1, 28.

Gobbels, M., and Spitznas, M. Corneal epithelial permeability of dry eyes before and after treatment with artifical tears. *Ophthalmology* 99 (1992): 873–78.

Lane, B.C. The Tear Film: Nutriture Considerations. Presented at the College of Syntonic Optometry Annual Conference, 1995.

Lockie, A. *The Family Guide to Homeopathy*. New York: Simon & Schuster, 1989, p. 166.

Mansour, A.M. Tolerance of topical preparations: Cold or warm? *Annals of Ophthalmology* 23 (1991): 21–22.

McLenachan, J. New aspects of the aetiology of Sjogrens Syndrome. *Transactions of the Ophthalmological Society* 76 (1956): 413–26.

Paterson, C.A. et al. Vitamin C levels in human tears. *Archives of Ophthalmology* 105 (1987): 376–77.

Simmons, P.A., Clough, S.R., Teagle, R.H., and Jaanus, S.D. Toxic effects of ophthalmic preservatives on cultured corneal epithelium. *American Journal of Optometry & Physiological Optics* 65 (1988): 867–73.

Talal, N. How to recognize and treat Sjogren's Syndrome. *Drug Therapy* (June 1984): 80–87.

Tsubota, K., and Nakamora, K. Dry eyes and video display terminals. *The New England Journal of Medicine* (February 25, 1993): 584.

Willis, R.M. et al. The treatment of aqueous deficient dry eye with removable punctal plugs. *Ophthalmology* 94 (1987): 514–18.

CHAPTER 6

Lockie, A. *The Family Guide to Homeopathy; Symptoms and Natural Solutions*. New York: Simon & Schuster, 1989, p. 161.

Moffat, J.L. *Homeopathic Therapeutics in Ophthalmology*. New Delhi: B. Jain Publishers, 1982, p. 126.

Randolph, T.G., and Moss, R.W. *An Alternative Approach to Allergies*. New York: Bantam, 1980, pp. 52, 111, 126, 142.

CHAPTER 7

1. Foos, R.Y., and Simons, K.B. Vitreous in lattice degeneration of retina. *Oph-thalmology* 91.5 (1984): 452–57.
2. Foos, R.Y., and Wheeler, N.C. Vitreoretinal juncture: Synchysis senilis and posterior vitreous detachment. *Ophthalmology* 89 (1982): 1502.

Other references used in this chapter

Akiba, J. Prevalence of posterior vitreous detachment in high myopia. *Ophthal-mology* 100 (1993): 1384–88.

Boldrey, E.E. Risk of retinal tears in patients with vitreous floaters. *American Journal of Ophthalmology* 96 (1983): 783–92.

Diamong, J.P. When are simple flashes and floaters ocular emergencies? *Eye* 6 (1992): 102–04.

Lane, B.C. Dietary & Nutriture Risk Factors for Change in Cataracts and Mac-ular & Vitreous Diseases. Presented at the College of Syntonic Optometry Annual Meeting, 1995.

Lane, B.C. Nutrition & vision. In *1984–85 Yearbook of Nutritional Medicine* , edited by J. Bland. New Canaan, CT: Keats Publishing, Inc., 1985, p. 239–81.

Lockie, A. *The Family Guide to Homeopathy*. New York: Simon & Schuster, 1989, p. 160.

Murphy, R. *Homeopathic Medical Repertory*. Pagosa Springs, CO: Hahnemann Academy of North America (HANA), 1993, p. 384.

Ueno, N. et al. Effects of visible-light irradiation on vitreous structure in the pres-ence of a photosensitizer. *Experimental Eye Research* 44 (1987): 863–70.

CHAPTER 8

1. Salov, L., and Fischer, W. *Hidden Secrets for Better Vision*. Fischer Publishing Co., Canfield, OH, 1995, p. 129–30.

Other references used in this chapter

Duke, J.A. *Handbook of Medicinal Herbs*. Boca Raton, FL: CRC Press Inc., 1985, p. 116.

Harper-Shove, F. *Prescriber and Clinical Repertory of Medicinal Herbs*. Essex, England: C.W. Daniel Co. Ltd., 1952, pp. 7, 40, 41.

Hooper, M. *Herbs and Medicinal Plants*. New York: Arco Publishing, 1986.

Jackson, M. and Teague, T. *The Handbook of Alternatives to Chemical Medicine*. Oakland, CA: Lawton-Teague Publications, 1975, p. 62.

PHP Clinical Guide. Portland, OR: Professional Health Products, 1992, p. 16.

Randolph, T.G., and Moss, R.W. *An Alternative Approach to Allergies*. New York: Bantam, 1980, pp. 52, 111, 126, 142.

APPENDIX

1. Gach, R.M. *Acupressure Potent Points*. New York: Bantam, 1990.

General Bibliography

Bensky, D., and O'Connor, J. *Acupuncture: A Comprehensive Text*. Seattle, WA: Eastland Press, 1981.

Cerney, J.V. *Acupuncture Without Needles*. New York: Parker Publishing Co., Inc., 1974.

Elias, J., and Ketcham, K. *The Five Elements of Self-Healing*. New York: Harmony Books, 1998.

Elias, J., and Masline, R.S. *Healing Herbal Remedies*. New York: Dell Publishing, 1995.

Maciocia, G. *The Foundations of Chinese Medicine*. New York: Churchill Livingstone, 1989.

Sardi, B. *Nutrition and the Eyes*, Volumes 1,2,3. Montclair, CA: Health Spectrum Publishers, 1994.

Xiangcai, X. *The Encyclopedia of Practical Traditional Chinese Medicine: Ophthalmology*. Beijing, China, 1990.

Glossary

Acupressure: Using finger pressure on acupuncture points to increase circulation in that area.

Acupuncture: The placement of needles into specific points on the body to increase energy flow.

Antioxidant: Any substance that donates an electron that quenches free radicals, preventing tissue aging and degeneration.

Aqueous humor: Watery fluid inside the front of the eye.

Base formula: A constitutional herbal formula used to balance out imbalances in specific organ systems.

Cataracts: Loss of clarity of the crystalline lens inside the eye.

Chronic simple glaucoma: Loss of peripheral vision with a normal drainage angle; also called open-angle glaucoma.

Conjunctivitis: "Pink eye." Inflammation of the white of the eye and/or the inner lining of the eyelid.

Cornea: Clear covering over the colored part of the eye; the most sensitive part of the body.

Essence: Extract of the vital energy of a flower or other substance.

Floaters: Shadows that appear to float in the vision, especially in bright light.

Free radical: Unpaired electron that will steal an electron from other molecules, damaging them (a process called oxidation).

Glaucoma: Peripheral vision loss due to loss of optic nerve fibers.

Homeopathy: Potentized (serial dilution and agitation) remedies prescribed according to similarity of symptoms.

Hypothyroidism: Low thyroid function.

Intraocular pressure: Fluid pressure inside the front of the eye.

Lens: Crystalline lens that changes focus of the eyes; densest protein in the body.

Macular degeneration: A deterioration in the central part of the retina, where the ability to see detail and color vision exists.

Meridians: Energy pathways that connect the various acupressure/acupuncture points and internal organs.

Osmolarity: Concentration of electrolytes.

Peripheral vision: Side vision, as opposed to central vision.

Qi: The Chinese word for energy that circulates through pathways in the body called meridians.

Retina: The photoreceptor layer in the back of the eye; the most electrically charged tissue in the body.

Sties: Local inflammation in eyelid, the thinnest skin in the body.

Tonometer: Instrument to measure eye pressure. (See intraocular pressure.)

Traditional Chinese Medicine: The style of medical practice that originated in China thousands of years ago based on the principles that health dysfunctions are due to imbalances of energies represented by five elements — water, wood, earth, metal and fire.

Yin/yang: Represent opposite but complementary qualities. A symbolic representation of a universal process that portrays a changing, rather than a static picture of reality.

Resources

OPTOMETRY/OPHTHALMOLOGY

Organizations

American Academy of Ophthalmology
Public Information Program
PO Box 7424
San Francisco, CA 94210-7424
(415) 561-8500
e-mail: ips@aao.org
Brochures and eye fact sheets on eye conditions and visual impairment.

American Foundation for the Blind
11 Penn Plaza, Suite 300
New York, NY 10001
(800) 232-5463

American Optometric Association
243 North Lindbergh Boulevard
St. Louis, MO 63141
(800) 365-2219

College of Optometrist in Vision Development (COVD)
353 H. Street, Suite C
Chula Vista, CA 92010
(619) 425-6191

The Foundation Fighting Blindness
Executive Plaza 1, Suite 800
11350 McCormick Road
Hunt Valley, MD 21031-1014
(888) 394-3937
(800) 683-5551
(410) 785-1414, 785-9687
(410) 771-9470 (fax)
Provides information for those with retinal degenerative diseases (such as macular degeneration and retinitis pigmentosa). Call one of the toll-free numbers for a listing of support groups in your area.

Glaucoma Support Network
Glaucoma Research Foundation
490 Post Street
San Francisco, CA 94102
(800) 826-6693
(415) 986-3162
e-mail: glaucoma@itsa.ucsf.edu
A national telephone network for glaucoma patients and their families. Support and encouragement from volunteers helps patients cope with vision loss from glaucoma. The Glaucoma Research Foundation sponsors and conducts research, provides patient education and support services, and publishes *Gleams* (a quarterly newsletter) and a patient guide about treatments, therapies and coping with glaucoma.

Lighthouse National Center for Vision and Aging
111 E. 59th Street
New York, NY 10022
(800) 334-5497
(212) 821-9713

Clearinghouse of support groups for visually impaired older people. Publishes a directory of self-help and mutual aid support groups and a newsletter. The Lighthouse Center for Education, another branch of this organization, provides information, resources, education and professionally prepared multimedia and print material for community education lectures. Technical consultations and catalog available.

Macular Degeneration Awareness
Education Support Group Against All Odds, Inc.
Contact: Morton Bond
700 S. Hollybrook Drive #210
Pembroke Pines, FL 33025
(305) 431-3111
Nonprofit organization providing awareness, education and support.

Macular Degeneration Foundation Education, Inc.
PO Box 9752
San Jose, CA 95157-9752
(408) 260-1335
fax: (408) 260-1336
e-mail: mdfeyes@aimnet.com
         eyesight@eyesight.com
Nonprofit corporation that provides a newsletter and other support services to the visually impaired.

National Eye Institute
Information Office
Building 31, Room 6A32
31 Center Drive MSC 2510
Bethesda, MD 20892-2510
(301) 496-5248
Provides publications on eye diseases and information on current eye research.

National Eye Research Foundation
910 Skokie Boulevard, Suite 207A
Northbrook, IL 60062
(800) 621-2258

Optometric Extension Program Foundation, Inc.
2912 South Daimler Street
Santa Ana, CA 92705
(714) 250-8070

Prevent Blindness America (formerly National Society to Prevent Blindness)
500 E. Remington Road
Schaumburg, IL 60173
(800) 331-2020
(708) 843-2020
Publishes a variety of information on vision, eye health and safety. Provides information on eye research and some community services.

Vision Improvement Practitioners

Beyond 20/20 Vision
Robert Michael Kaplan, O.D.
RR 2, S26C39
Gibson, British Columbia
V0N1V0 Canada
(604) 885-7118
fax: (604) 885-0608
Vision improvement products (books, tapes) and workshops.

Cambridge Institute for Better Vision
Martin Sussman
65 Wenham Road
Topsfield, MA 01938
(800) 372-3937
(508) 887-3883
Programs for better vision and catalog for vision improvement products.

Institute of Visual Healing
Grace Halloran, Ph.D.
655 Lewelling Blvd. #214
San Leandro, CA 94579
(510) 357-0477
Alternative and innovative treatments for retinitis pigmentosa, macular degeneration and glaucoma.

ULT
Jacob Liberman, O.D. Ph.D.
PO Box 520
Carbondale, CO 81623
(800) 815-4448
(303) 927-0100
fax: (303) 927-0101
Innovative light technology, vision nutrition products and workshops.

Eye Vitamin Suppliers

Supplements can be purchased at health food stores and pharmacies, but as quality varies incredibly, it is best to ask a qualified professional, herbalist, holistically trained M.D., naturopath or sophisticated health food store proprietor which companies are ethical and manufacture quality products. The number of manufacturers is vast, and they vary depending on which part of the country you live in.

Advanced Medical Nutrition Inc.
2247 National Avenue
PO Box 5012
Hayward, CA 94540
(800) 654-4432

Akorn, Inc.
Brand name: *OcuCaps*
Abita Springs, LA 70420
(800) 535-7155

Bronson Pharmaceuticals
1945 Craigh Road
St. Louis, MO
(800) 732-3323

Hickey Chemists
Brand name: *Macula*
1645A Jericho Turnpike
New Hyde Park, NY 11040
(800) 724-5566

Integral Health Apothecary
3 Paradise Lane
New Paltz, NY 12561
(888) 403-5861
fax: (914) 255-0036

LaHaye Laboratories
Brand name: *I Caps Plus*
801 Evergreen Point Road
PO Box 67
Medina, WA 98039-0067
(800) 451-1302

Lederie Consumer Health Division
Brand name: *Protegra*
Pearl River, NY 10965

Medical Ophthalmics Inc.
Brand name: *MaxiVision*
40146 U.S. Hwy. 19 North
Tarpon Springs, FL 34689
(800) 358-7791

Metabolic Maintenance Products
  Brand names: *VitalEyez*
  68994 North Pine Street
  Box 3600
  Sisters, OR 97759
  (800) 772-7873

Naturade Products, Inc.
  Brand name: *Eye Support*
  7110 Jackson Street
  Paramount, CA 90723
  (310) 531-8120

Nature's Herbs
  1113 North Industrial Park Drive
  Orem, UT 84059
  (800) 437-2257

Nature's Plus
  Brand name: *Ocucare*
  548 Broad Hollow Road
  Melville, NY 11747-3708
  (516) 294-0030

Numark Laboratories, Inc.
  Brand name: *Lipotriad*
  PO Box 6321
  Edison, NJ 08818
  (800) 338-8079

Nutri-West
  One Commercial Drive
  PO Box 109
  Florida, NY 10921
  (914) 651-1040

Physiologics
    Brand names: *Optivision, Bilberry*
    6565 Odell Place
    Boulder, CO 80301-3330
    800-765-6775

Quantum
    Brand name: *See*
    Box 2791
    Eugene, OR 97402
    (503) 345-5556

Solaray
    Brand name: *Vizion*
    2815 Industrial Drive
    Ogden, UT 84401
    (800) 669-8877

Starfire International
    Brand name: *Foresight*
    PO Box 4991
    Hilo, HI 96720
    (888) 889-7882
    website: http://www.star-base.net

Storz Opthalmics
    Brand name: *Ocuvite*
    3365 Tree Court Industrial Blvd.
    St. Louis, MO 63122
    (800) 325-9500

Twinlab
    2120 Smithtown
    Ronkonkoma, NY 11779
    (516) 467-3140

Vision Research Technologies
Brand name: *CataRx*
1025 Northern Blvd.
Roslyn, NY 11576
(516) 627-4102

Eye Drops

Conjunctisan A Eye Drops
VitOrgan
PO Box 4240
7302 Ostfildern 1 (Rult)
Fed. Rep. of Germany
Phone (07011) 4 48 12-0

Similisan #1, #2
Similisan Corporation
1321-D South Central Ave.
Kent, WA 98032
(800) 426-1644

Succus Cineraria
Walker Pharmaceutical Company
Luy Ties Pharmacal
4200 Laclede Avenue
St. Louis, MO 63108
(914) 255-3728

Thera Tears
Advanced Vision Research
7 Alfred Street, Suite 330
Woburn, MA 01801
(800) 579-8327

Viva-Drops
Vision Pharmaceuticals
Mitchell, SD 57301
(800) 325-6789

Recommended Readings

Bates, W.H. *The Bates Method for Better Eyesight Without Glasses.* New York: Henry Holt & Co./Owl Books, 1981.
Berne, Samuel. *Creating Your Personal Vision.* Santa Fe, NM: Color Stone Press, 1994.
Kaplan, Michael R., M.D. *Seeing Beyond 20/20: Improve the Quality of Your Vision and Your Life.* Hillsboro, OR: Beyond Words Publishing, 1987.
Lieberman, Jacob. *Take Off Your Glasses and See.* New York: Crown Publishers, 1995.

NUTRITION

Organizations

International Academy of Nutrition and Preventative Medicine
PO Box 18433
Asheville, NC 28814
(704) 258-3243

Recommended Readings

Wright, Jonathan, M.D. *Dr. Wright's Guide to Healing with Nutrition.* New Canaan, CT: Keats Publishing, Inc., 1990.
Hoffer, Abram, M.D. and Walker, Morton. *Orthomolecular Nutrition,* rev. ed. New Canaan, CT: Keats Publishing, Inc., 1978.
Lieberman, Shari and Bruning, Nancy P. *The Real Vitamin and Mineral Book.* Garden City, NY: Avery Publishing Group, Inc., 1990.

ACUPUNCTURE

Organizations

American Association of Acupuncture and Oriental Medicine (AAAOM)
433 Front St.
Catasauqua, PA 18032-2506
(610) 433-2448
Both the AAAOM and the NAAOM (see below) offer referrals to qualified
practitioners in your area and can provide information on qualifications for
licensing and certification in each state.

National Alliance of Acupuncture and Oriental Medicine (NAAOM)
638 Prospect Ave.
Hartford, CT 06105
(203) 586-7509

National Commission for the Certification of Acupuncture (NCCA)
1424 16th St. NW, Suite 105
Washington, DC 20036
(202) 232-1404
Offers a list of fully certified acupuncturists (those who have graduated from
an accredited school, with a minimum of three years postcollege training and
passed the NCCA comprehensive exams) in your area.

National Council of Acupuncture Schools and Colleges (NCASC)
PO Box 954
Columbia, MD 21044
(301) 997-4888

Recommended Readings

Worsley, J.R. *Acupuncture: Is It for You?* New York: Harper & Row, 1973.

Beinfield, Harriet, L.Ac. and Korngold, Efrem, L.Ac., O.M.D. *Between Heaven and Earth: A Guide to Chinese Medicine.* New York: Ballantine Books, 1991.

Elias, Jason and Ketchum, Katherine. *The Five Elements of Self-Healing.* New York: Harmony Books, 1998.

Mitchell, Ellinor R. *Plain Talk About Acupuncture.* New York: Whalehall, Inc., 1987.

Kaptchuk, Ted. *The Web That Has No Weaver: Understanding Chinese Medicine.* New York: Congdon and Weed, 1992.

HERBAL MEDICINE

Organizations

American Botanical Council and the Herb Research Foundation
    PO Box 201660
    Austin, TX 78720
    (800) 748-2617
    (800) 373-7105

American Herb Association
    PO Box 1673
    Nevada City, CA 95959
    fax: (916) 265-9552

Herb Research Foundation
    1007 Pearl Street, Suite 200
    Boulder, CO 80302
    (303) 449-2265

Buying Herbs by Mail

The following is a list of reputable dealers who grow and sell organic dried herbs, both in bulk or in capsules, tinctures, etc.

Avena Botanicals
PO Box 365
West Rockport, ME 04865

Frontier Cooperative Herbs
Rte. 1, Box 31
Norway, IA 52318

Gaia Herbs
62 Old Littleton Road
Harvard, MA 01451

Green Terrestrial
PO Box 41, Rte. 9W
Milton, NY 12547

Herbalist and Alchemist
PO Box 458
Bloomsbury, NJ 08804

Herb Pharm
PO Box 116
Williams, OR 97544

Island Herbs
c/o Ryan Drum
Waldron Island, WA 98297

ITM Herb Products
2017 SE Hawthorne
Portland, OR 97214
(800) 544-7504

Mountain Herbals
104 Main Street
Montpelier, VT 05062

Starfire International
PO Box 4991
Hilo, HI 96720
(888) 889-7882
website: http://www.star-base.net

Chinese Herbs And Patent Remedies

If your city has a Chinatown or a Chinese section, there is bound to be a Chinese herbal shop where all of the patent remedies we suggest can be found. You can also get these herbs from:

Crane Enterprises
45 Samoset Avenue
RFD #1
Plymouth, MA 02360

Integral Health Apothecary
3 Paradise Lane
New Paltz, NY 12561
(888) 403-5861
fax: (914) 255-0036

ITM Herb Products
2017 SE Hawthorne
Portland, OR 97214
(800) 544-7504

Starfire International
PO Box 4991
Hilo, HI 96720
(888) 889-7882
website: http://www.star-base.net

For health professionals, or sizable orders of Chinese bulk herbs and prepared herbal products:

Mayway Trading Co.
622 Broadway
San Francisco, CA 94133
(415) 788-3646

North-South China Herbs
1556 Stockton Street
San Francisco, CA 94133
(415) 421-5576

Tai Sang Trading Co.
1018 Stockton Street
San Francisco, CA 94108
(415) 981-5364

For Chinese herbal products manufactured in the United States for health
practitioners:

Brion
12020-B Centralia Road
Hawaiian Gardens, CA 90716

East-Earth Herbs
PO Box 2082
Eugene, OR 97402

Health Concerns
2236 Mariner Square Drive #103
Alameda, CA 94501

K'an Herbs
2425 Porter Street, Suite 18
Soquel, CA 95073

Meridian
17 St. Saveur Court
Cambridge, MA 02138

Planetary Herbs
Box 533
Soquel, CA 95073

Seven Forests
2017 SE Hawthorne
Portland, OR 97214

Tea Garden Herb Emporium
1344 Abbot Kinney Boulevard
Venice, CA 40291

Zand
PO Box 5312
Santa Monica, CA 90405

Recommended Readings

The American Herb Association Newsletter. PO Box 353, Rescue, CA 96672.
Elias, Jason and Masline, Ryan Shelagh. *Healing Herbal Remedies.* New York: Bantam Doubleday Dell, 1995.
Castleman, Michael. *The Healing Herbs.* Emmaus, PA: Rodale Press, 1991.

HerbalGram. American Botanical Council, PO Box 201660, Austin, Texas 78720. (512) 331-8868, (800) 373-7105, fax: (512) 331-1924.

Tierra, Lesley. *The Herbs of Life.* Freedom, CA: Crossing Press, 1992.

Medical Herbalism. PO Box 33080, Portland, OR 97233.

Hoffmann, David. *The New Holistic Herbal.* Rockport, MA: Element Books, 1992.

NEHA Newsletter, Northeast Herbal Association. PO Box 146, Marshfield, VT 05658-0146.

NATUROPATHY

Organizations

American Association of Naturopathic Physicians
601 Valley Street
Seattle, WA 98109
(206) 298-0126

National College of Naturopathic Medicine
11231 SE Market Street
Portland, OR 97216
(503) 255-4860

Physicians

Naturopathic physicians are well trained in vitamin, mineral and herbal methods of healing, as well as Western medical physiology and pathology. Send a SASE to the address below and request a listing of certified naturopathic physicians in your area.

American Association of Naturopathic Physicians
601 Valley Street
Seattle, WA 98109
(206) 298-0126

Recommended Readings

Murray, Michael, N.D. and Pizzorno, Joseph, N.D. *Encyclopedia of Natural Medicine.* Rocklin, CA: Prima Publishing, 1991.
Murray, Michael, N.D. and Pizzorno, Joseph, N.D. *Textbook of Natural Medicine, Vols. 1–2.* Seattle: John Bastyr College Publications, 1989.

HOMEOPATHY

Organizations

The American Institute of Homeopathy
925 East 17th Ave.
Denver, CO 80218
(505) 989-1457

The Connecticut Homeopathic Association
PO Box 1055
Greens Farms, CT 06846

Foundation for Homeopathic Education and Research
2124 Kittredge Street
Berkeley, CA 94704
(510) 649-8930

Homeopathic Academy of Naturopathic Physicians
14653 South Graves Road
Mulino, OR 97042

National Center for Homeopathy
801 North Fairfax, Suite 306
Alexandria, VA 22314
(703) 548-7790

Homeopathic Pharmacies

All sell homeopathic remedies, some by kit, some by single remedies, most by both. Many supply other homeopathic products as well, from books to tapes to software.

Arrowroot Standard Direct
    83 East Lancaster Avenue
    Paoli, PA 19301
    (800) 234-8879

Biological Homeopathic Industries
    11600 Cochiti Southeast
    Albuquerque, NM 87123
    (505) 293-3843

Boericke and Tafel
    2381 Circadian Way
    Santa Rosa, CA 95407
    (707) 571-8202

Boiron-Borneman, Inc.
    6 Campus Boulevard, Bldg. A
    Newtown Square, PA 19073
    (610) 325-7464

Boiron-Bourneman, Inc.
    98c West Cochran
    Simi Valley, CA 93065
    (805) 582-9091

Dolisos
    3014 Rigel Road
    Las Vegas, NV 89102
    (702) 871-7153

Hahnemann Medical Clinic Pharmacy
828 San Pablo Ave.
Albany, CA 94706
(510) 527-3003

Homeopathic Educational Services
2124 Kittredge St.
Berkeley, CA 94704
(510) 649-0294

Longevity Pure Medicines
9595 Wilshire Boulevard, #502
Beverly Hills, CA 90212
(310) 273-7423

Luyties Pharmacal
4200 Laclede Avenue
St. Louis, MO 63108
(314) 533-9600

Medicine from Nature
10 Mountain Springs Parkway
Springville, UT 84663
(801) 489-1500

New Vistas
5260 East 39th Street
Denver, CO 80207
(800) 283-4533

Santa Monica Homeopathic Pharmacy
629 Broadway
Santa Monica, CA 90401
(310) 395-1131

Similisan Corporation
(Similisan #1, #2 eye drops)
1321-D South Central Ave.
Kent, WA 98032
(800) 426-1644

Standard Homeopathic Company
204-210 West 131st Street
Los Angeles, CA 90061

Washington Homeopathic Products
4914 Del Ray Avenue
Bethesda, MD 20814
(800) 336-1695

Recommended Readings

Cummings, Stephen, M.D. and Ullman, Dana, M.P.H. *Everybody's Guide to Homeopathic Medicines.* Los Angeles: Jeremy P. Tarcher, Inc., 1991.

Lockie, Andrew. *The Family Guide to Homeopathy: Symptoms and Natural Solutions.* New York: Prentice Hall Press, 1993.

Ullman, Dana. *Homeopathic Medicine for Children and Infants.* Los Angeles: Jeremy P. Tarcher, 1992.

Cook, Trevor. *Homeopathic Medicine Today: A Study.* New Canaan, CT: Keats Publishing, Inc., 1989.

Panos, Maesimund B., M.D. and Heimlich, Jane. *Homeopathic Medicines at Home: Remedies for Everyday Ailments and Minor Injuries.* Los Angeles: Jeremy P. Tarcher, 1981.

McCabe, Vinton. *Let Like Cure Like.* New York: St. Martin's Press, 1997.

CHIROPRACTIC

Organizations

American Chiropractic Association
1701 Clarendon Boulevard
Arlington, VA 22209
(703) 276-8800

Association for Network Chiropractic Spinal Analysis
PO Box 7682
Longmont, CO 80501
(303) 678-8086

International Chiropractors Association
1110 North Glebe Road, Suite 1000
Arlington, VA 22201
(703) 528-5000

World Chiropractic Alliance
2950 N. Dobson Road, Suite 1
Chandler, AZ 85224
(800) 347-1011

OSTEOPATHY

Organizations

American Academy of Osteopathy
3500 DePauw Boulevard, Suite 1080
Indianapolis, IN 46268
(317) 879-1881
fax: (317) 879-0563

American Osteopathic Association
142 East Ontario Street
Chicago, IL 60611
(312) 280-5800

LIGHT THERAPY

Organizations

College of Syntonic Optometry
1200 Robeson Street
Fall River, MA 02720-5508
(508) 673-1251

Dinshaw Health Society
100 Dinshaw Drive
Malaga, NJ 08328
(609) 692-4686

Environmental Health and Light Research Institute
16057 Tampa Palms Boulevard, Suite 227
Tampa, FL 33647
(800) 544-4878

Society for Light Treatment and Biological Rhythms
PO Box 478
Wilsonville, OR 97070
(503) 694-2404

Practitioners

ULT
Jacob Liberman, O.D. Ph.D.
PO Box 520
Carbondale, CO 81623
(800) 815-4448
(303) 927-0100
fax: (303) 927-0101
Innovative light technology, nutrition products and workshops.

Products

Environmental Lighting Concepts
Full Spectrum Light Products
3923 Coconut Palm
Tampa, FL 33619
(800) 842-8848

Recommended Readings

Ott, John, D.Sc. *Health and Light*. Old Greenwich, CT: The Devin-Adair Co., 1988.

Dinshaw, Darius. *Let There Be Light*. Malaga, NJ: Dinshaw Health Society, 1985.

Liberman, Jacob. *Light: Medicine of the Future*. Santa Fe, NM: Bear & Co. Publishing, 1993.

AUTHORS' RESOURCES

Integral Health Apothecary
3 Paradise Lane
New Paltz, NY 12561
(888) 403-5861
fax: (914) 255-0036
The Integral Health Apothecary is the pharmacy connected with Integral Health Associates, a group practice in New Paltz, New York, whose aim is to treat the "whole person" utilizing various alternative and traditional healing modalities. Nutrition, acupuncture, herbal medicine, homeopathy, psychotherapy, chiropractic, natural vision care (by author Marc Grossman, O.D.), yoga, bodywork and massage therapy are practiced by experienced health care professionals. At our health and wellness center, we have established a pharmacy carrying a complete line of herbal (both Western and Chinese) products and supplements, as well as books and other related products. We can prepare tinctures for the prescription wanted, and we carry a full line of quality herbal tinctures and Chinese patent herbal remedies, as well as all the supplements mentioned in this book.

Starfire International
PO Box 4991
Hilo, HI 96720
(888) 889-7882
website: http://www.star-base.net
Starfire is a nonprofit distribution network co-founded by Dr. Swartwout and Mr. John Moylan. Starfire distributes health products developed by Dr. Swartwout and other leading natural health practitioners. Benefits of a $30 lifetime membership include a health information Launch Kit complete with a video on cutting edge health technologies, an informative monthly health newsletter with frequent feature articles by Dr. Swartwout and access to wholesale pricing on many of his most frequently recommended products. Members can also earn commissions through referrals. Health practitioners and health food stores also participate on a national provider panel to provide products and services to members through the network.

Remission Foundation
    900 Leilani Street
    Hilo, HI 96720
    800-788-2442
    International 808-935-5086
    Founded by Dr. Glen Swartwout, the Remission Foundation is dedicated to the advancement of natural vision and health care. Based in Hilo, Hawaii, Remission Foundation maintains an active research clinic which provides health consulting services for clients worldwide. A catalog of recommended self-help health products based on Dr. Swartwout's research in Biological Medicine and Vision Care is available for a suggested donation of $5. A free information packet about health consulting services is available free upon request.

Index